SAVED *by* ANGELS

EXPANDED EDITION

SAVED *by* ANGELS

to share how **GOD** talks to everyday people

EXPANDED EDITION

BRUCE VAN NATTA

DESTINY IMAGE® PUBLISHERS, INC.

P.O. Box 310, Shippensburg, PA 17257-0310

"Promoting Inspired Lives."

This book and all other Destiny Image, Revival Press, MercyPlace, Fresh Bread, Destiny Image Fiction, and Treasure House books are available at Christian bookstores and distributors worldwide.

For a U.S. bookstore nearest you, call 1-800-722-6774.

For more information on foreign distributors, call 717-532-3040.

Reach us on the Internet: www.destinyimage.com.

ISBN 13 TP: 978-0-7684-4134-5

ISBN 13 Ebook: 978-0-7684-8827-2

For Worldwide Distribution, Printed in the U.S.A.

2 3 4 5 6 7 8 / 17 16 15 14 13

DEDICATION

THIS BOOK IS DEDICATED TO THE LIVING TRIUNE GOD. MAY HIS name be glorified in these pages, and may the people who read this book come to know Him better.

ACKNOWLEDGMENTS

I WOULD LIKE TO EXPRESS MY GRATITUDE TO EVERYONE AT DEStiny Image Publishers for doing the work of the Lord. May He bless you as you bless others. I thank all of the people who encouraged and helped me throughout this project and continue to do so. From the group who proofread the manuscript, to the prayer warriors, to the people who gave me advice, information, and insight, you all are God-given treasures. I owe a special thanks to my family for their constant support and love. May the sacrifices you have made, due to this project and ministry, be a testimony to God's love.

CONTENTS

PREFACE

A FEW MONTHS BEFORE MY ACCIDENT, WHEN A TRUCK FELL ON me nearly killing me, I had just finished writing this book. The project had taken over three years, and after I was done, I began exploring publishing options. Several times in this book, I use the cartoon illustration of the devil on one shoulder and an angel on the other. This analogy turned out to be very descriptive of my experience throughout my accident and recovery. In fact, the parallels between the events of the accident and what I had already written in the book are shocking. My accident and the miracles that surrounded it are a perfect example of what this whole book is about. God performed these great miracles so that people would take note of this message!

Before my escape from death, the Lord had done many other miraculous things in my life, starting when I was very young. But it took over 30 years before I started to feel comfortable sharing them. Due to all the mistakes that I have made and the way that I lived much of my life, I never felt worthy to tell anyone about God. But God kept after me. I documented these God occurrences over the years and then put them into book form only after the Lord repeatedly prompted me to do so. For several years, God also kept telling me that He wanted me to go into full-time ministry, but I enjoyed doing things my own way and had made up my mind that I would not.

Then the truck fell on me, and God sent His angels to miraculously save my life so that I could and would share a message from Him to you. God loves each and every one of us, regardless of who we are or what we've done. He communicates specifically with everyone and desires to have an intimate relationship with each of us. If we choose not to listen to Him, He continues to reach out to us, but eventually we will reap the consequences of disobedience in our lives. I pray that our Lord blesses and nurtures everyone who has the opportunity to read this book and to ponder its relevance to their lives. I pray that my words may be like the apostle Paul's:

> *When I came to you, brothers, I did not come with eloquence or superior wisdom as I proclaimed to you the testimony about God. For I resolved to know nothing while I was with you except Jesus Christ and Him crucified. I came to you in weakness and fear, and with much trembling. My message and my preaching were not with wise and persuasive words, but with a demonstration of the Spirit's power, so that your faith might not rest on men's wisdom, but on God's power* (1 Corinthians 2:1-5).

INTRODUCTION

THE EVENTS OF NOVEMBER 16, 2006, CHANGED MY LIFE FOR-
ever. I will never forget what happened on that day; it will be with me
as long as I live. Many of us can think of defining moments in our
lives. Sometimes they are marked by tragedy, sometimes by triumph;
rarely are they marked by both. But this was one of those uncom-
mon days.

I was a self-employed diesel mechanic who performed on-site
repairs. On this particular day, I was at a customer's shop about 45
minutes from my home. The vehicle that I was working on was a
Peterbilt logging truck. I had worked nearly 12 hours that day in order
to complete my portion of the engine repairs, and I was just finishing
up. I had been working with the driver of the truck, and after we put
the engine back together, we began checking it over and testing the
repairs. The rest of the truck had not been completely reassembled,
but the driver planned on finishing the remaining work the next day.
I began to put my tools back into the tool boxes on my service truck
as the semi engine ran up to operating temperature. The driver asked
me, since I was there, if I could also diagnose a non-related oil leak
before I left. I was in a hurry to get home, but I thought this task
would only take a few extra minutes.

I rolled underneath the front of the truck feet first on a creeper
and started wiping off the area that appeared to be leaking. All of

a sudden, the truck fell off the jack and crushed me against the concrete floor. The front axle had come down across my midsection like a blunt guillotine, the five to six tons of weight nearly cutting me in two. From my viewpoint, it looked and felt like I was cut in half as there was less than an inch of air space between the axle and the cement on my left side and about two inches of space on my right side. In a moment of panic, I tried to bench press the ten thousand plus pound mass off of me. When reality set in, I realized the gravity of the situation and called out "God help me!" twice. I listened as the truck driver called 911. When he got off the phone, I begged him to shut the engine off because the vibration of the engine directly above me was transmitted through the axle and right into my body. Small amounts of blood started to come out of my mouth when I tried to talk. I watched as the driver repositioned the jack and raised the truck up off of my body. I was scared of it falling again, and I wanted to get out from underneath that truck in the worst way. The large chrome front bumper was just behind my head, and I reached both hands back and grabbed the bottom of it. It took all the strength that I had for me to pull myself far enough that my head was out from underneath the truck. I stayed conscious long enough to see the first person who responded to the 911 call.

The next thing I remember, I was at least 10 or 15 feet above the scene, looking down at myself and the whole situation. The strangest part about my "out-of-body" experience was feeling like I was just an observer to what was happening below me. It was as if I was watching a movie. I felt no emotion, only a sense of peace. I heard one man say to another that there was no way I was going to live, and it didn't matter to me one way or another. From my viewpoint, I could tell that my body was still mostly under the truck but that my head was sticking out from under the front bumper. I could see that my eyes were closed and that my head was turned toward the driver's side of the truck. The man I had been working with was on his knees above me and was crying and patting me on the head as he was talking to me. I could hear and understand every word he said.

The most incredible thing wasn't that I was having this experience; it was what I saw next. On either side of my body were twin angels, also on their knees, facing the front of the truck. From my vantage point, I was watching from above and behind them. The driver of the truck is over six feet tall, yet the heads of these angels were at least a foot and a half taller than his head. If they would have been standing up, I think they would have been close to eight feet tall. They had very broad shoulders and looked to be extremely muscular. There were no wings. Each angel had positioned his arms under the truck, angled toward my body. The angels had ringlets of long blond hair that fell at least half way down their backs. They were wearing white or ivory robes. It was hard to tell the exact color because of a yellowish light surrounding each angel. They seemed to be glowing. I also noticed that the robe fabric was very unusual. It was a woven material, but the thread size was very large, like miniature rope. It appeared to be very strong and durable. The angels never moved; they were as steady as statues. I couldn't see their faces because my view was from behind them, but from what I could see, they were identical in appearance.

LIFE OR DEATH

More people began to come to the scene of the accident, and I continued to watch from above. A red-haired emergency worker arrived, talked to someone, and walked up the driver's side of the truck. She moved the truck driver out of the way and asked him my name. She held my head, patted my cheeks, and told me to open my eyes. She kept repeating herself in a loud voice, and the next thing I knew, I was no longer watching from above but was looking at her through my own eyes. She told me that it was very important for me to keep my eyes open. I thought about what she was saying and realized that I had been out of my body until she got me to open my eyes. This made me believe that what she said was true and important; I was on the verge of death! Then I thought about the angels that I had seen. I looked where they had been, but I could see nothing there now with my human eyes.

As I lay there, I heard a voice in my head telling me to shut my eyes and just give up. When I did shut my eyes, the incredible pain stopped, and I could feel my spirit drifting away from my body. But there was also another voice; this one was quieter, more like a whisper. It told me that if I wanted to live, I would have to fight, and it would be a hard fight. It was almost as if the red-haired emergency worker could hear that voice too because she then asked me what I had to fight for. All I could think of was my wife and four children. These two voices, or conflicting thoughts, volleyed back and forth in my head. If you think of that old cartoon with the devil on one shoulder and an angel on the other, you can use it to picture what was happening. The louder voice that was telling me to give up and die was not from God, but the whispering voice that told me to fight was. As always, the devil promotes death and God promotes life. It's also interesting to note that God will always tell us the truth. He warned me that it was going to be a hard fight, and it has been. It seems that, most often, the right choice is not the easiest one.

I was transported by ambulance to a local hospital and then flown to our state's largest trauma center. I stayed awake the whole time, fighting to hang on and refusing to close my eyes. When the emergency doctors starting scanning my body, they were astounded. There were so many injuries that they couldn't decide where to start or what to do. They had given me several units of blood, but it just kept leaking out into my stomach cavity. As they were sliding me back in for another CAT scan, everything started to go dim for me, and although I hadn't been able to talk for quite a while, the Lord gave me the strength to tell them that I was going to die and that they had to do something right now. The doctors told me several weeks later that, as soon as I said that, both numbers in my blood pressure reading dropped out of sight! They removed me from the machine and rushed me to the operating room.

The doctors operated on me only long enough to reattach the veins and arteries that had been severed. The head trauma surgeon had been called in from home. He told my family that, in all his years as a trauma doctor, he had never seen anybody so badly traumatized and still be alive. He told my family that he was going to cross his fingers and wait at least six hours to see if I was still alive before he would operate on me again. My wife told him that he could cross his fingers but that she and others were going to pray for my life. The prayers were answered, and the doctors resumed operating on me the next morning. They had to remove most of my small intestine and perform various other repairs to combat my several internal injuries. They decided not to do anything with the two vertebrae that were spider cracked in my spine; they would try to let them heal on their own.

The next thing I remember was waking up a few weeks later. I had had three operations during that time, and my wife never left my side. The night of my accident, she was at our children's school for parent-teacher conferences. When she got home and heard the news, she dropped to her knees and turned it all over to God, knowing that He would give her the strength to get through whatever lay ahead. The only thing that she took with her to the hospital that night was her Bible. To everyone's amazement, I was sent home a little more than a month after the accident. But after a few days, I was back in the hospital with severe complications stemming from a damaged pancreas and spleen.

I spent a few more weeks in the hospital, but I got out long enough to spend the Christmas holidays at home. Then I returned to the hospital. This cycle repeated itself a few times, and then the doctors decided that they would have to perform another major operation. They had to remove another section of my small intestine that had died and was almost completely closed off. We were told that an adult needs a minimum of 100 centimeters of small intestine to be able to live by eating food. I was already down to this critical minimum length before my fourth operation, and then they removed more. Before the accident, I weighed over 180 pounds; three months afterward, I was already down to 126 pounds because of the inadequate amount of small intestine left in my body.

MORE MIRACLES

Nine months after the accident, I was at the hospital for some tests in preparation for my fifth operation. While performing the procedure, the radiologist and his supervisor found that I now have at least one third, or around 200 centimeters, of small intestine. (We have since found out that there is actually even more, about one half or 300 centimeters.) When they looked at the doctors' notes from the previous operations, they found that they had recorded a total length of 100 centimeters several times during the first three operations and this was before removing more in my fourth operation. It was hard for them to believe that the head of the trauma department and other doctors had made multiple mistakes on my chart and in their calculations, since these men are at the top of their field and have a spotless reputation.

Upon further research the before and after x-rays and CAT scans show that they didn't make any mistakes. Something had happened that the doctors couldn't explain. Intestines had come out of nowhere, but how?

What the doctors didn't know was that several people had been praying for me and that a man named Bruce Carlson had flown in from New York to pray over me after my fourth operation. This man has often displayed the gift of healing, and the Lord has used him to heal hundreds of people. The Bible tells us that we, as Christians, are to pray with expectation for sick people to be healed. Sometimes God chooses not to heal someone in the method or timetable that we want, but that is His decision, not ours. As believers, we are told to pray with expectation, and the results are up to God. When Bruce Carlson prayed over me that day, he put one of his palms on my forehead. He asked the Lord to answer all of the prayers that people had been praying for me, and when he said that, I felt something like electricity flowing from his palm and into my body. He prayed for my small intestine to supernaturally grow in length in the name of Jesus, and as he did, I could feel something wiggle around inside my stomach. Of course, I didn't know for sure that my intestine had lengthened until the radiologist told me a few months later.

It has now been a few years since my accident and I have almost no side effects or physical problems at this point, despite the tremendous amount of trauma that my body incurred. My weight has also climbed back up to about 170 pounds, thanks to the added intestine. Now that more time has passed, the doctors have also told me just what a miracle it is that I am alive. They said that, because of the arteries and veins that were completely severed, I should have bled to death internally in about eight to ten minutes or less. Rather, it was over two and a half hours from the time that I was injured until they started to operate on me! They also told me that according to an extensive study that had been done on the subject a few years before my accident, I am the only case that doctors know of where a person has had major arteries severed in five places in the chest and still lived. All other cases have come in dead on arrival. I told my doctors that I know why I am still alive. I got to see the two angels that saved my life!

HIS WILL BE DONE

We can now see how the Lord was able to accomplish His plans despite this tragedy and bring good from bad so that His name would be glorified in the end. Right from the beginning of this nightmare, my wife and I have clung to the promise that God gives us in Romans 8:28, "And we know that in *all* things God works for the good of those who love Him, who have been called according to His purpose."

It is too early to see all of the good things that God has planned to come out of this tragedy, but we can already see some things clearly. We have seen our faith grow by leaps and bounds due to this event. We are now closer to the Lord than we have ever been. Our family is more compassionate toward the needs and problems of others. I have become more patient than I used to be. Our home church has rallied together to support our family in a way that many senior members of the church have told us has never happened in the past. Some people who were not involved actively in church or prayer life have been drawn back to the Lord again or for the first time. Some have said that the accident has caused a small revival in our community and we see the same impact wherever we tell the story. Many have accepted Jesus as their Lord and Savior and many more have been healed and set free.

When I tell people about seeing the angels who saved my life it has permanently affected many of them. It makes it hard for even skeptics to argue with the reality of these miracles when they are shown the medical facts. More than once, I have seen people break down in tears after hearing this story because it touches them deep inside. People are affected when confronted with the truth of God's reality, mercy, and love. Because of the power of this testimony and to be obedient to God we have founded Sweet Bread Ministries, which is now our full-time work. We travel around the world telling others what God has done for us and what He will do for them. Listeners are compelled to consider the reality of God, angels, healing, and most importantly their salvation. Many people report being healed of all kinds of sicknesses, diseases, addictions, and emotional issues after attending one of our meetings. What a blessing it is to see God do miracles in other people's lives. It is clear to us that, although this accident started out as a tragedy, the Lord has used it to bring triumph for His Kingdom.

CHAPTER 1

GOD TALKS TO EVERYDAY PEOPLE

GOD TALKS TO EVERYDAY PEOPLE—EVERY DAY. ARE YOU AN "everyday person"? Do you go about your days doing what needs to be done—working, playing, eating, sleeping—and doing the same the next day? Everyday people are people you pass on the street, see in the grocery store, sit beside at church, and meet for lunch. They can be any age or color; it matters not. God wants a personal relationship with each of us. When Jesus walked the earth, He lived with and communicated with everyday people. From fishermen and prostitutes to kings and social outcasts, He loved all people. He wanted everyone to know how great His Father's love was for them, and He went to extremes to show that love. Today, 2,000 years later, His goal remains the same.

The religious leaders of Jesus's day wanted to know why He associated with common sinners. He told them in Luke 19:10, "The Son of Man came to seek and to save what was *lost*." He also told them in Matthew 9:12-13, "It is not the healthy who need a doctor, but the *sick*. But go and learn what this means: 'I desire mercy, not sacrifice.' For I have not come to call the righteous, but *sinners*." None of us are sinless, but God remains faithful to His children who ask for forgiveness. First John 1:8 says it this way: "If we claim to be without sin, we deceive ourselves and the truth is not in us." It is easy to believe that one sin is worse than another, but the Bible tells us that *all* sin separates us from God. Romans 3:23 says, "For *all* have sinned and fall short of the glory of God."

Even so, God still talks to His people—His creation—because He loves us. It's been that way since the beginning, and it is still that way today. The Bible tells us in Malachi 3:6, "I the Lord do not change." In Hebrews 13:8, it says, "Jesus Christ is the same yesterday and today and forever." Because God has created each of us uniquely, He uses different ways to talk to us. If we were to examine every instance in the Bible when the Lord communicates with someone, we would find that they could all be listed under one of the following categories. Each of these seven categories will be discussed within the book. God talks to us through:

1. The process of prayer.

2. The Bible or other written words.

3. The spoken word of clergy or others.

4. An inner whisper or audible voice—the Holy Spirit.

5. Design and circumstances, sometimes called "fate" or "coincidence."

6. Dreams and visions.

7. Angels.

Because God can and does talk to people in all of these ways, we know that He is listening to us.

The question is, are *you* listening to *Him*? Throughout history, there have been countless examples of God reaching out to people. No matter your social or economic status, your religion, your race, or your circumstances, God loves you, and He wants you to know that His Son Jesus died for you so that you can live forever with Him in Heaven. That is the simple truth. But very often people have a lot of questions. What should we believe? Who should we believe? What religion or denomination is the "right" one? Is there really a God? If there is a God, why did He let this or that happen? I don't have all the answers, but the more that I read the Bible, the more answers are revealed to me. All we really need to know is that God loves us—the remaining questions will be answered during our eternal life with Him. As Paul said:

> *For we know in part and we prophesy in part, but when perfection comes, the imperfect disappears. When I was a child, I talked like a child, I thought like a child, I reasoned like a child. When I became a man, I put childish ways behind me. Now we see but a poor reflection as in a mirror; then we shall see face to face. Now I know in part; then I shall know fully, even as I am fully known* (1 Corinthians 13:9-12).

Even though, by nature, I am a doubter, I have no other choice but to believe in God. After all, He has talked to me through all of the seven ways on the list. Please look at that list again. Pretty incredible, isn't it? Many people may think that this is too far-fetched or even that it is impossible to believe. The doubting part of my nature would like to agree, but I can't. The Lord has communicated and continues to communicate with me, an everyday person, so frequently that I can't deny Him. Let me say right now I have not done anything to deserve God's attention. On the contrary, I have made some horrible mistakes and many bad decisions (maybe like you). Although I am not worthy of God's love, He loves me anyway. I'm grateful that He doesn't use "good enough" or "holy enough" standards toward us. Our only requirement for salvation is to believe in Him and to believe that Jesus died for our sins. Acts 4:12 says, "Salvation is found in no one else, for there is no other name under heaven given to men by which we must be saved."

God talks to you, even if you don't have faith in Him or His Son Jesus. Stop right now and think about the times in your life when you received what you needed at just the right time. Keep thinking; there are more. Maybe it was a phone call, an opportunity, or maybe it was a friend or a spouse. Maybe you received help when you thought no one cared. Did you chalk it up to coincidence or fate? Could it be that God was helping you, reaching out to you, loving you? What about the times that you made a really bad decision or a big mistake? Did someone or something try to warn you? Think about it. Did God try to talk to you through a person, a sign, or a nagging thought? God wants the best for us, but we have to be willing to listen and to obey Him. Sometimes it is hard to listen. There are so many distractions, so many things pulling us in different directions.

OUR CHOICE

Picture again in your mind the cartoon with an angel on one shoulder and a demon on the other. The character in the middle isn't important because he could be any of us. The Bible tells us that this is an accurate picture of life. We are told that both angels and demons exist. Angels do God's work, and demons do the devil's work (see Matt. 13:38-40). If you are like me, it's hard to believe in things you can't see, not impossible, but hard. In the same way that God uses different methods to talk to us, the devil uses different tactics too. Oddly enough, they both use a lot of the same methods to communicate with us. The big difference is that God loves us and always tells us the truth while the devil hates us and lies to us. But don't be discouraged; God tells us that He will triumph over evil (see Rom. 16:20).

Before you read further, please stop and pray to God. Pray that He would give you a believing heart, a wise heart. Pray that God would give you an open mind to hear His voice and His truths and the discernment to realize which thoughts are from Him. The Bible tells us in James 1:5-6, "If any of you lacks wisdom, he should ask God, who gives generously to all without finding fault, and it will be given to him. But when he asks, he must believe and not doubt, because he who doubts is like a wave of the sea, blown and tossed by the wind." Be glad because God also tells us in Isaiah 41:9-10, "I have chosen you and have not rejected you. So do not fear, for I am with you; do not be dismayed, for I am your God. I will strengthen you and help you; I will uphold you with My righteous right hand."

Maybe you've already been praying to God, or maybe not. Maybe you've been asking God for a miracle, a sign, or an answer. Maybe you are not sure if there is a God or if He is listening to you. Maybe you're still weighing the odds, still waiting, still watching to see what will happen in your life before you make a decision about believing in God.

I want to tell you about someone I know. Bob (not his real name) and I used to work together. Bob was having some troubles in his life. The exact troubles don't really matter. They could be the same kind of troubles that you and I have, everyday problems. He had consulted doctors and talked with counselors, but the problems remained. Talking hadn't helped and neither did the medicine. These problems started to affect his work, and because I was his supervisor, I called him in to my office, and he told me what was wrong. I truly felt sorry for this man, and I knew that God was the only one who could help him. I asked if he believed in God, and he said he did but that he hadn't been to church since he was young. I asked if he had tried praying, he said he hadn't thought about it. We decided to pray right then and there. After a few hours, I went to visit him in his work area to ask how it was going. "No change," he said sadly. I expected him to say better, or at least a little bit better. I was puzzled and frustrated. What went wrong? (I have to admit that God has spoiled me in my prayer life; I think, because of my stubbornness, He has had to go the extra mile to reach me.)

I immediately went to an area where I could be alone to pray. I prayed for this man and asked God to answer. He did! Instantly, He brought the story of the Samaritan woman at the well to my mind. I didn't know what the relevance was, but I knew I had to tell Bob. The story is found in John 4:1-42. Here is my paraphrase. One day, Jesus and His disciples were traveling through Samaria and stopped at a well near a town. Jesus stayed at the well while the disciples went to town for food. A local woman came to get water from the well and Jesus asked her for a drink. She was surprised that He spoke to her because Jews didn't associate with Samaritans. Jesus told her that, if she knew who was asking her for a drink, she would have asked Him for "living water." He told her that anyone who drank this water would never thirst again. She asked Him to give her some of this water so that she would not have to come to the well anymore.

Jesus told her to go get her husband and come back, but she said she had no husband. Jesus told her that she was right in saying that she had no husband, because she had been married five times, and the man she was with now was not her husband. Because He knew her past, the woman thought He was a prophet and asked Him where the correct place to worship was. He told her that the important thing was to worship God in spirit and in truth. She told Him that the Messiah was coming someday and that He could answer her question. Jesus told her that He was the Messiah. She believed what He said and went back to town to get others to talk to Him. The

Bible says that many people became believers over the next two days while listening to Jesus.

While telling Bob the story, I realized what God was trying to tell him (and us). Before God can truly help us, we need to admit our sin and humble ourselves before Him. Second Chronicles 7:14 says "If My people, who are called by My name, will humble themselves and pray and seek My face and turn from their wicked ways, then will I hear from heaven and will forgive their sin and will heal their land." I suggested to Bob that he go to a place where he could be alone, confess his sins to God (known and unknown), ask God for forgiveness, and ask God for His help. I'm happy to tell you that a short time later, Bob was back in my office, telling me that he had prayed again and that this time he felt like a very heavy weight had been lifted from him. I gave him a daily devotional to take home, and he even went to church that Sunday. On Monday at work, he told me that "coincidently" the sermon had been about the Samaritan woman at the well.

If you can relate with Bob's situation, if you've been to the end of your rope and think that God may not be listening to you, or that He doesn't care, or maybe doesn't even exist, I pray that you follow the four steps from Second Chronicles 7:13-22 that lead to forgiveness and fellowship with Him.

1. Humble yourself before God, and admit your sin. (Proverbs 3:34 says, "He mocks proud mockers but gives grace to the humble.")

2. Pray to God, asking for forgiveness. (First John 1:9 says, "If we confess our sins, He is faithful and just and will forgive us our sins and purify us from all unrighteousness.")

3. Earnestly seek God. (Romans 10:13 says, "Everyone who calls on the name of the Lord will be saved.")

4.   Turn from sinful behavior by yielding your life to Christ. (First Peter 2:16 says, "Live as free men, but do not use your freedom as a cover-up for evil; live as servants of God.")

I would love to tell you that, if you follow these four steps, everything will turn out for you as you wish every time, but I can't. Sometimes God's will is not our will, and sometimes His timetable is not ours. At those times, all we can do is trust Him and believe His promises. His plan is always better because He is all-loving, all-knowing, and sovereign. Jeremiah 29:11 says, "'For I know the plans I have for you,' declares the Lord, 'plans to prosper you and not to harm you, plans to give you hope and a future.'"

KEEPING TRACK

After each of the following chapters in this book, you will find an area where you can write the times and ways that God has talked to you. This book came into being because of a similar journal, or list, that I started more than ten years ago. I was debating with some friends the question of whether there was a God or not, and I couldn't remember all of the things God had done in my life. So the next day, I wrote down everything I could remember and kept the list in my wallet. Over time, I added to it as more things happened. Documenting the "God incidents" in my life has been an invaluable tool in my walk with the Lord for two reasons. It strengthens my faith when I look at the list of things He has done already, and it helps me when I tell other people why I believe. I have seen God use this simple list to help bring people into a saving faith in Him and to help current Christians deepen their faith and grow closer to Him.

The things on my list that God has done for me are the same kind of things that He is willing to do for anyone who wants to have a real relationship with Him. Our Lord truly desires to have a relationship with each of us—an intimate, "best friend" kind of relationship. When this kind of relationship is a reality in our lives, we begin to know and experience our Lord in deeper and more fulfilling ways than ever before. My prayer for you is that you would use this book as a tool to help you realize how much God loves you and to help see what He has done in your life—how He is reaching out to you, how He is talking to you, and how He is building a relationship with you. May God's name be glorified every time you realize that God has been talking to you—even before you were listening or seeking Him! As God tells us in Isaiah 65:24, "Before they call I will answer; while they are still speaking I will hear."

JOURNAL

_____

_____

_____

_____

_____

_____

_____

_____

_____

_____

_____

_____

_____

_____

_____

_____

_____

_____

_____

_____

_____

_____

CHAPTER 2

GOD TALKS THROUGH THE PROCESS OF PRAYER

JESUS TELLS US IN MATTHEW 21:22, "IF YOU BELIEVE, YOU WILL receive whatever you ask for in prayer." If you didn't just fall out of your chair, please reread that verse again. I don't know about you, but that promise is a little hard to swallow for some of us. Not only did Jesus say that, but in the previous verse He said, "I tell you the truth…you can say to this mountain, 'Go, throw yourself into the sea,' and it will be done" (Matt. 21:21). How could Jesus say such things? Clues are found at the beginning of both verses: "I tell you the truth, if you have faith and do not doubt…" and "If you believe…." For our prayers to be answered, we have to have faith in Him and His ability and power. We have to believe that He can and will do what's best for us and those we love. Whatever we are praying for needs to be for our good or for someone else's good; and most importantly, our prayers need to be in line with God's will.

Let me ask you a question: If you pray to win the lottery, for your team to win a game, or for something similar, could you honestly pray without having any doubt? Is it possible that someone else needs money more than you do? Is it possible that there is a bigger reason why the other team needs to win? God wants to answer our prayers, but He also wants our prayers to be in line with His will. When we pray, we can't just demand what we want. We must first ask God what His will is and what He wants for us.

GOD ANSWERS PRAYERS

You read previously about the list that I have been keeping. I also mentioned that I think God has been spoiling me in my prayer life. When I first started sharing these "God talking" stories with other people, it bothered me that many people did not have the same experiences as me or that they often did not realize it when they did. Since then, I have found several other Christians with stories just like mine. And I have come to the conclusion that God often talks to us when we need Him the most, but if we aren't listening, we can't hear Him. Time and again, God has used tragedy to bring people closer to Him. Sometimes we don't cause the tragedies in our lives, but if you're like me, we often do.

My prayer life started because of an incident when I was five years old, and it is the first thing I can think of that proved to me the reality of God. I didn't tell anyone this story for more than 20 years after it happened. My wife was the first person I told, and since then, it has become somewhat easier for me to share with others. The only time I remember going to Sunday school as a small child was the time when I went with my grandpa and grandma. Their church was a small country church, and after the service, the children went to the basement for Sunday school. Because I was new to the group, the teacher had me sit beside him. Three other children sat around the table with us.

The lesson for the day was about the time when people were bringing children to Jesus so that He could touch them. His disciples were trying to chase the children away so they could attend to more important things. Jesus became angry and told His disciples to let the children come (see Matt. 19:13-15). The Sunday school teacher told us that this proved how much Jesus loved children and that we could be sure that He would listen to us when we prayed. I remember thinking that, even though I could tell the teacher sincerely believed this story, I wasn't so sure.

During that time in my life, my father was a truck driver and my mother also worked outside of the house. Because I was young, sometimes I had to stay with another family until my parents got home from work. This meant that I had to occasionally spend the night there also. The other family had a boy and a girl who were older than me. The parents had a lot of pornographic magazines and watched pornographic movies. Sometimes they would get drunk, perform sexual acts with each other, and then involve us kids in their perversion. They told me that this was a secret, and if I told my parents, they would be very angry. After awhile, I discovered that certain things felt good. One day, when we had guests at our house, I was showing one of the visitors a "trick" that I learned at my babysitter's home. My mom caught me in the act and asked where I had learned such a thing. I told her that the babysitter's son showed me—I never did tell on the parents. Not long after that, my mom found me putting on her makeup. Mom said she was going to tell Dad everything as soon as he returned home.

I remember listening through the door to the conversation between my mom and dad in the kitchen late that night. I can't tell you how bad and dirty I felt. My parents were very upset because they didn't understand why I hadn't told them what had been happening, and they were afraid for my future. I felt deep in my heart that everything was entirely my fault and that I was truly a bad person. Then I remembered what the Sunday school teacher had said about Jesus answering our prayers. (I'm sure now that it was the Holy Spirit reminding me.) I decided right then that even if praying didn't work, I had nothing to lose. For those of you who have children, or if you can remember being a child, what I prayed for that day will make sense to you. I prayed that Jesus would come and give me a hug; I just wanted to be comforted. Instantly, there was a bright light, and I felt His arms around me, holding me. It felt as if I was being dipped in liquid love, from the top of my head to the bottom of my feet. I could no longer hear my mom and dad's distraught conversation. Everything else was gone except for the most awesome feeling of pure love. I fell asleep in Jesus's arms that night. Even though this happened a long time ago, I can still remember just how good it felt. Jesus tells us in Matthew 11:28, "Come to me, all you who are weary and burdened, and I will give you rest."

My next answered prayer was not as dramatic, but it still impressed on me the power of prayer. When I was 7 or 8 years old, it was a rule in our house that we were not allowed in our parents' closet. I broke the rule and found a baseball in the closet. I thought it would be fun to play with, so I decided to go outside and toss it around where I wouldn't be seen. I had fun throwing it up on the roof of our barn and then trying to catch it when it rolled back down. This was working fine until I threw it a little too hard and it went over the peak and down the other side of the barn. In the front of the barn, the grass was mowed, but on the back side, the weeds and grass were as tall as me. I looked for the ball through the tall grass for hours that day and couldn't find it. I looked for hours again the next day and still couldn't find it.

On the third day, I looked in the morning until lunchtime, but still I found no ball. I was starting to panic because my dad was expected home soon. I was afraid of getting into trouble for going into the closet and for losing the ball. After lunch, on my way back out to the barn, I remembered how God had answered my prayer a few years earlier. I prayed that He would help me find the ball. This time I walked into the tall grass and immediately found the ball. I told God "thank you" and promised Him that I wouldn't take it again. Although this might sound like a small thing, it was another steppingstone in my walk to trust God.

When I was 14, my 5-year-old brother was diagnosed with cancer. The doctors told my parents that there was a good chance my brother would die. While my parents were at the hospital, I stayed home with my other younger brother. After a few days, my parents decided that we all needed to go be with my little brother at the hospital because he might never come home. I refused to go. My parents were angry with me, but they finally gave in and allowed me to stay home. I didn't tell my parents, but the reason I wanted to stay home was so that I could pray for my brother alone, as I had done in the past. Because God had answered my two other prayers, I was sure He would answer me this time also.

I got out a Bible, looked up various words and promises in the index, and then wrote on a piece of paper the exact location of the passages by chapter and verse. Then I began to pray. I told God that these were His promises, not mine. I also told Him that because I had seen His power before, I knew that He could answer my prayer. I asked Him to heal my brother completely. When I got done praying that night, I knew with all of my heart that God was going to heal my brother. Over the following weeks and months, my brother's cancer disappeared, and he never even lost his hair during the treatments. Although I'm sure a lot of people had been praying for my brother, I felt that God would have healed him even if I had been the only one who had prayed—not because of any merit of my own but because I knew God could and would answer prayer. I didn't know it at the time, but the Bible tells us that faith in God is a gift (see 1 Cor. 12:4-11). Through my previous experiences, God had nurtured this gift. I still have that piece of paper with the list of verses, and I have used it many times over the years to remind myself of God's power and love.

WRONG DIRECTION

During high school, I started making some pretty bad decisions. One of those bad decisions led to me getting a girl pregnant. She had taken a home pregnancy test, and it proved positive. We went to a local health agency, and their test results were the same. They told us our different options, and we left. We knew that we didn't want to have an abortion, but we didn't know what we were going to do. After I dropped her off at home, I went back to my house and called on God once again. I started praying at about 7 o'clock in the evening and didn't stop until about 9. I told God I was sorry. I asked for His forgiveness and help. I told Him that I didn't think I was old enough to be a dad but that I would quit school and try. I also told Him that if there was any way He could change the situation or somehow undo what we had done, that I would rather have that. My girlfriend called later that night and said she had had a miscarriage.

This showed me that when we make mistakes, God still loves us and will answer our prayers although not always in the way we hoped. It also showed me that there are often serious consequences to our sin. If you think you have made too many mistakes, or too big of a mistake, for God to love you or to answer your prayers, think again. I know that some people reading this will have a hard time accepting what I believe happened. I have to tell you that, although I wasn't ready to be a father, after the miscarriage, I felt just as much punishment as relief. We read in Second Samuel 11-12 about a time when God did much the same thing with His servant David. David had stolen another man's wife and then had him killed. The woman became pregnant, and after the child was born, God took the child's life as a punishment for what David had done. Some may think that this was not fair to the child, but who can know the future or the mind of God? It is quite possible that it was more merciful for God to take the lives my unborn child and

David's son to a perfect heaven, than to let them grow up in the situations they were created in.

ADDICTED

Later on, I had one particular girlfriend for several years. We got engaged and were going to get married after we finished college. Unfortunately, I got involved with drugs, and what started out as fun turned into a serious drug addiction. I used drugs to numb the pain I felt inside, which was caused by different things that had happened during my childhood. The drugs gave me a sense of peace; unfortunately, this kind of peace only lasted until the drugs wore off. My drug addiction caused my girlfriend and me to have many fights, and eventually she ended our relationship. For two years, I tried to fill the hole left in my life with more drugs and alcohol. Although I decided not to date anyone, there were a few "one night stands" during that period, but I never got serious about any of them.

One particular night, I had planned to go out drinking with my roommate as usual, but when the time came, I didn't want to go. I was feeling depressed and just wanted to hide in my bedroom. As strange as this might sound to some people, I had decided that praying to God was only for emergencies, for those times when I couldn't do something on my own or control my own circumstances. This was an emergency. I went to bed that night and prayed. I prayed that God would send me a mate, someone who would love me no matter what, someone who would love me even with all of my problems.

During this time, I raced studded motorcycles on ice. I was supposed to have a race the next day, but my motorcycle was broken, so I went to the races with my friends as a spectator. While at the races, I saw Lori, a high school classmate. We said "hi," but nothing more. After the races, they awarded the trophies to the winners at a nearby tavern that had sponsored the races. One of my friends and

I decided to stay and have a few drinks. We had our first drink and started to play a game of pool when I looked toward the bar and saw Lori. It looked as though a bright light was shining on her. I asked my friend if he thought she was sitting under a light. He gave me a funny look and said, "No, why would you say that?" I decided to get another drink and see if she was sitting under a recessed light. When I got there, I saw that there were no lights in the ceiling above her.

I didn't realize that God was showing me my future wife because I didn't think she was my type. We small-talked for a little while, and then I went back to my pool game. A short time later, I looked her way again and this time it seemed as if her teeth were glowing. I asked my friend if he saw the blonde's teeth glowing. He told me that I had had two too many drinks. Nevertheless, I asked Lori that night for a date the following week. It took me a few weeks to realize that Lori was God's answer to my prayer for a mate and that was why I was the only one who could see her glow. Now, after enjoying each other for more than 18 years and having four beautiful children together, I continue to thank God that He knew she was my type. God is good!

After nearly a year of dating, Lori and I decided to get married, and we set a date. I am a mechanic by trade, and I didn't think that the job I had at a local garage would provide enough to support us. I thought that if God was so willing to answer my crisis prayers, He might be just as willing to answer prayers about everyday needs. I took that chance and prayed for a better job. The next week, while I was at a training class in another town, one of the people there offered me a job that I couldn't refuse. Lori and I changed our wedding date, got married, and moved to the other town.

I hate to admit that it took me over 20 years to realize that God was there for me all the time, no matter how big or small the problem. I suppose sometimes I'm not a very quick learner. How about you? Because God had been so faithful, I began to call on Him more and more, and He continued to outperform my expectations! He tells us in Philippians 4:6, "Do not be anxious about anything, but in everything, by prayer and petition, with thanksgiving, present your requests to God."

EVERYDAY LIFE

After being married awhile, my wife and I decided to get a dog. We hoped to have kids within a few years, so we wanted a dog that would be good with kids. We decided to pray for a good family dog. Shortly after praying, a friend from work told us that he had one puppy left from a recent litter. The puppy's tail was broken because it had been caught in the kennel door. Apparently, nobody had picked her because of her crooked tail. We knew right away it was the answer to our prayer. We brought her home. As it turned out, Eve was an excellent dog, exceptionally smart, easy to train, good with our kids, and a good protector. God saved the dog with a crooked tail just for us so that we could have a better dog than we even hoped for. If we had gone dog shopping, without first praying about it, we probably wouldn't have picked this dog, but because we prayed first, God provided the dog that was best for us. God talks through answered prayer!

When I met Joe (not his real name) at work, he was like most of us, struggling to make ends meet. He had just saved up enough money to buy a second vehicle so that his wife could have a car. A short time later, she wrecked the car. He told me about the accident and the details just didn't seem to make sense. When I questioned him, he called his wife, and she admitted to him that she had been with another man when she had the accident. He was devastated, and I felt terrible about raising the questions. Over the next few weeks, things got worse at home, and he finally moved out and moved into a barn. One day, as I walked by the truck he was working on, I noticed that he was underneath the truck crying. I stopped and thought about what to say to him to make him feel better, but all I could focus on was how crappy it was for his wife to do what she had done.

As I stood there, the silence became uncomfortable, and I decided to ask God to give me something good to say to Joe. Instantly, God gave me a couple of Bible verses to share. We talked about God a little, and Joe stopped crying. He thanked me for talking with him. That night, on his way to the barn, Joe stopped at a church. No one was there, but he went inside anyway and prayed to God. On his way out, he grabbed a daily devotional. When he got back to the barn, he read the material. The same Bible verses that I had shared with him earlier were the verses listed for that day's devotion!

When I pulled into the parking lot the next morning, I saw Joe sitting in his vehicle. This surprised me because he was usually five or ten minutes late. He got out of his truck with the devotional in his hand and asked me if I had read it the day before. I told him no and asked him why it mattered. He told me the story about stopping at the church. He went on to say that if the things I had told him the day before were just a canned message, they were of no value. I explained to him that I had prayed to God to give me something comforting to tell him and that God told me what Scripture verses to share with him. I also told him that the devotional that he was holding wasn't the one that I used. In fact, it was from a completely different church denomination. Joe found these facts hard to believe.

I'm sorry to say that, by this point, I was angry, and I went into work, leaving Joe standing there in the parking lot. It didn't matter, though, because God had proved His point to Joe already. He was reaching out to Joe, showing him His love. I praise God often for having the power (and patience) to use someone as imperfect as I am to do His work. Joe ended up realizing that God did indeed give me those verses for him and then prove it by putting those same verses in the devotional. Joe came to faith in God and was even a Sunday school teacher for a few years. Joe and his wife reconciled, but only long enough for him to bring her into God's family. Sometimes God has eternity in mind, not just the here and now.

After a few years, the business where I was working was sold and moved to a nearby town. I went from being a lead man at the first place, to being the dayshift foreman at the second place. God was blessing us greatly. We started having children, and we bought a house closer to my new job. Because we believe in tithing (we give God the first 10 percent of my gross wages), and because of the added expenses of children and an old house, we sometimes found ourselves in financially tight times. I prayed and asked God to provide more money for us to live on. The next day at work, my supervisor was fired because of some inappropriate actions. The owners of the company asked me to fill in for the manager position until a replacement could be hired. I did, and was offered the job shortly thereafter, which I accepted.

As always, God answered my prayer with more than I even expected. The owners treated me very well and taught me a great deal about people and business. They were Christian men, and I respected them very much (and still do). Thankfully, they had a lot of patience and took the time to explain things to me. God blessed me with a lot of technical ability that I drew on as a mechanic. Due to this, I had been able to do my old job with ease. My new position was another story. I had very little supervisory skills, and most of my employees were older then me. As such, I didn't feel very confident as manager and often avoided confrontation that would have benefited my department. Although I couldn't count on myself, I knew I could count on God, and it was at this point in my life when I began depending on Him more and became closer to Him.

When our department didn't have enough work to keep the mechanics busy, I would go somewhere private and ask God to send work. Sometimes, before I finished praying, the phone would start ringing. If we had a job we couldn't figure out, I would pray for guidance to help us fix the problem. When we couldn't fill a position,

I would pray, and God would send someone. I finally realized just how much I depended on God to help me every day. It still puzzles me how God can be so faithful to us when we are not always faithful to Him. I know I'm not perfect, and yet God continues to talk to me through the process of prayer.

HIS FAITHFULNESS

The next experience could have been cited in Chapter 7, on dreams and visions, or in Chapter 5, on the Holy Spirit, but I tell it to you now because it was an answered prayer. As our children got older, they spent more time outside. We lived near a busy major highway, and after one of the children was almost hit by a car, we decided we wanted to build a house in a more rural area. We spent more than a year looking at house plans and searching for a piece of land off the beaten path. We finally found the perfect spot and a house plan that would accommodate the six of us.

After talking to the bank and adding up the costs, we realized that we wouldn't be able to afford it with my current income. My annual review was coming up soon, so I decided to tell my boss about the situation beforehand. I explained to him that I was going to need a $5,000 annual raise to follow through with our family plans. He didn't make any promises but said that he would think about it and would give me an answer during my review. I told my wife that, if he didn't grant my request, I was going to quit. Unfortunately, I am a stubborn (sometimes bullheaded) person. I would like to say that I'm just determined, but that would be a lie.

The night before my review, I decided to pray about it just in case I hadn't convinced my boss on my own. That night I had a dream (or vision) of my review. I could see myself, my boss, and the human resources person sitting in the HR office. I heard my boss say that he was going to give me $2,500, and then I woke up. I was mad at first, but then I realized that God was trying to talk to me. The Little Whisper in my head (the Holy Spirit) said to not be foolish but to be patient. In the morning, I told my wife my dream and what the Little Whisper had said. I knew that God was preparing me for the outcome of the review. That day at the review, my boss gave me a $2,500 bonus check but no raise. If God had not given me the dream (or vision), I would have turned in my two-week notice on the spot because that is what I had made my mind up to do. Although God had not given me what I wanted, He still answered my prayer by giving me the dream and telling me to be patient.

Not long after this happened, my mother-in-law had some rather serious health concerns. Because Lori is an only child, she felt that we should move home as soon as possible. Although I wanted to move out of our house, I wasn't sure about moving back to our hometown area because it has a rather depressed economy. I was afraid of not being able to support our family on one income. Lori and I wanted her to be able to stay home with our children and to not have to work outside the home, so I didn't know what to do. I knew that, if I left my job, there wasn't anybody currently working in my department that could take over the manager responsibilities. Even though my boss had not given me what I wanted, I still felt a deep sense of gratitude to the owners, and I didn't want to see the company suffer. I prayed to God and told Him that if it was meant for us to move home, that He needed to provide my replacement at work and a job back home for me. Within a week, He gave me both answers.

A few years before, a man had told me about an employee who used to work for him. He raved about him and said that if I ever had the chance to hire him, I should. Two days after I prayed for my replacement, this man applied for a mechanic's position. I took a chance and told him when I hired him that I had prayed for my replacement and that I felt that God had sent him. I told him about my secret plans to leave in about a year and that I would start training him right away. Because the owners didn't know I was planning to leave, we would have to do it undercover. I started making a complete list of my everyday routines. I also noted all the mistakes that I had made so the new guy could learn from my mistakes. The final list I made was of all the changes that I thought should be made to make the department more profitable. Some of these changes were drastic, so the owners would have to make those decisions.

I was a little nervous about how the owners would react if I told them I was planning on leaving in a year, so I waited until there were only three months left, and then I told them. I gave the owners my resignation notice, and then I told them that I had prayed for my replacement and that God sent this man. I was surprised when they told me that I had no business looking for my replacement. They put ads in the paper and posted the job internally. When all was said and done, they agreed with God and replaced me with the man I had trained. In the meantime, I was asked for an analysis of the department. I gave them the list I had already created, and after they conducted their own investigation, they made many of the changes I had suggested. During the training period for my replacement, I often prayed to God that He would help this man do a much better job than I had done and that the department would be more profitable for the owners. After I left and this man took over, I would periodically call for an update. After a year, I stopped calling because it was obvious that he was doing better than I had done. Have you ever heard the statement, "Be careful what you pray for or you just might get it"?

THE TRUCK

When I had originally prayed for God to send a replacement and a job back home, I had expected to get a job similar to the one I had (as a manager). This was not God's plan. A few months before that prayer, I had asked the used-vehicle manager at work to find me a different vehicle. My old minivan had close to 300,000 miles on it, and I thought it was time for something more reliable. I told him that I wanted a small, two-wheel-drive pickup. Months later (five days after I prayed about a job back home), the used vehicle manager said he had a truck for me and that I should test drive it by taking it home that evening. When I first saw it, I thought he was joking. It wasn't even close to what I had asked him for. Because I didn't want to be rude, I drove the truck home that night and showed my wife.

While looking at the truck that evening, I realized that it would be very easy to turn it into a work truck. I could take off the pickup box and put on a utility body with no other modifications. It already had heavy springs, a long wheel base, and was a four-wheel drive. Because I had been a mechanic for a long time, I already owned a lot of tools. That night, I came to the conclusion that this was how God was answering the second part of my prayer. I could use this truck and my tools to start a mobile repair service. After we moved home, that's exactly what we did, and God blessed our business from the start.

I began to see how God could use me even more than He had before because of the flexibility of owning my own business. There have been many opportunities for me to do His work because of the position He has provided for me. For instance, my workload dropped off immediately upon starting to write this book. This was actually one of the reasons I knew how much He wanted me to get it done. While working on this project, one of my constant prayers has been that God would use me as His pen to write His words to you.

GOD ANSWERS PRAYERS

The experiences I have shared with you in this chapter are only a few of the many times that God used the process of prayer to shape me and speak to me. Following the advice of First Thessalonians 5:17 and Philippians 4:6 I now try to pray continually about everything, but as I have already shared, it has not always been that way. Early in my Christian walk a fellow doubter once told me that it wasn't right for me to keep a list of answered prayers if I didn't also keep track of the times that God didn't answer my prayers. Because of that person, I also kept that list for a few years as well. I can tell you that there were only a relatively small number of things written on that list because at that point in my life I only prayed about "big" things. Some of the things on that list were there because God didn't answer me in the time frame that I prayed for. In fact a few of those prayers weren't answered for several years. For instance one took over twenty years to come to pass and there was a "selfish" prayer that took thirty years before it was just recently answered. Another prayer on that list is there because God let the exact thing happen that I was praying *wouldn't* happen. I saw later that this was for my own good. The last items on that list were there because they were apparently not God's will and therefore didn't get answered in the way I wanted. I have to be honest and tell you that I still don't understand why God did not grant some of these prayers, but I have come to realize that He knows better than I do and we can trust him even when we don't understand Him.

For those of you who have prayed for something, and you think that God hasn't heard you or listened to your prayer, please reread the four steps listed near the end of Chapter 1. We may not always get the answers we want, but God *will* answer. I know from personal experience that, when you have previously seen the power of God in action and then He doesn't respond to one of your prayers, it can be very frustrating. During those times, and during all times, we have to trust that God has a better plan. It has been said that sometimes one of God's best gifts is not answering a certain prayer. Because only God knows the future, only He knows what is truly best for us, and others, in the long run. God is still speaking through the process of prayer even when we don't get the answer we want.

One of the most import things we need to realize about prayer is that God has designed it to be a process or interchange. It is not meant to be a one-way street, but a two-way street. In other words we should not believe that it is just a simple monologue where we send our messages up to God hoping He hears us, but we should expect a dialogue where there is communication back and forth.

This means that as we pray we need to then "be still" as Psalm 46:10 says and listen for God to speak back to us. I think the analogy of a telephone call works very well to describe this give and take, two entities communicating back and forth. The problem is that many people pick up the phone, dial God's number and then just keep talking until they hang up and walk away, never giving the Lord a chance to say anything. Most of us wouldn't dream of doing this to our friends or loved ones, yet we do it to God all the time. God loves us so much He wants to spend time with us, loving on us, just like a best friend or close family member would.

If you have never tried praying to God, I encourage you to try. God is faithful, and He answers prayers—even prayers from common sinners like you and me. James 5:17-18 says, "Elijah was a man just like us. He prayed earnestly that it would not rain, and it did not rain on the land for three and a half years. Again he prayed, and the heavens gave rain, and the earth produced its crops." I think God enjoys showing people how much He loves them and how powerful He is. My guess is that the only thing He enjoys more than that is seeing people respond to His love. Jesus tells us in Matthew 7:7-11:

> *Ask and it will be given to you; seek and you will find; knock and the door will be opened to you. For everyone who asks receives; he who seeks finds; and to him who knocks, the door will be opened. Which of you, if his son asks for bread, will give him a stone? Or if he asks for a fish, will give him a snake? If you, then, though you are*

evil, know how to give good gifts to your children, how much more will your Father in heaven give good gifts to those who ask Him!

YOUR TURN

Write about the times in your life when God talked to you by answering your prayer. Write about the times when God talked to you by *not* answering your prayer or by giving you an answer other than the one you originally wanted.

_____

_____

_____

_____

_____

_____

_____

_____

_____

_____

_____

_____

_____

STUDY QUESTIONS

1. Let's say you became separated from a loved one in an enormous crowd of people. Could you recognize their voice in the crowd? Why? What about the voice of a stranger? Why? Now read John 10:27 and John 8:47. What does this teach us about our relationship with God? How can we recognize His voice better? (For a clue look at the title of the next chapter.)

2. Read through some of the Bible's promises about our relationship with God and record the verb phrases or actions of the believer for each listed reference and then what the Lord does in response. For example the answer for the first reference would be, "We are to call upon, go, pray to, seek, search with all our heart and then the Lord will listen to us, be found by us, gather us and bring us back from captivity.—Jeremiah 29:11-14; 2 Chronicles 16:9a; John 6:35; John 6:45. After looking at these action phrases evaluate your current walk with the Lord and see if they describe your relationship with God at this time.

3. Why does God use the analogy of a husband and wife to describe our relationship with Him? (See John 3:16; Revelation 3:20; Revelation 19:7-9.)

4. What is this relationship with God supposed to look like? What does the Bible teach us? Read Matthew 22:37-38 and Ephesians 5:22-33.

5. The Bible tells us that God talks to us through the process of prayer (see 2 Chron. 7:14). What examples of this can you find in the Bible? What patterns of prayer are shown in the Bible?

    Prayer is not a one-way street, but a give-and-take relationship. It should be a dialogue not a monologue.

6.   What does First Thessalonians 5:17 say about prayer? How about Philippians 4:6? Why?

Throughout the entire process of prayer God is proclaiming His love and faithfulness to us; He is speaking to us as we have relationship with Him.

JOURNAL

CHAPTER 3

GOD TALKS THROUGH THE BIBLE

GOD KNEW FROM THE BEGINNING THAT YOU AND I—EVERYDAY people—would need His help in this life. Because He loves us and cares about us, He gave us an instruction manual, the Bible. The first part of the Bible, the Old Testament, was written before Jesus was sent from Heaven. It tells us about how and why God created the earth, the sea, the animals, and humankind. The second part of the Bible, the New Testament, was written after Jesus's death. It is written by those who knew Jesus and/or were His followers. Many of the events within the Holy Scriptures have been proven true and accurate by religious scholars as well as by secular scientists and historians.

Some people have told me that they can't believe what the Bible says because it is just a gathering of letters written by men. While a portion of their reasoning may be correct, the Bible tells us in Second Peter 1:20-21, "Above all, you must understand that no prophecy of Scripture came about by the prophet's own interpretation. For prophecy never had its origin in the will of man, but men spoke from God as they were carried along by the Holy Spirit." So, the

Bible is not just a collection of stories or man-made ideas about God. Although each writer wrote from his own personal context (cultural background, education, style, language, etc.), they were all inspired by God through the Holy Spirit to write whatever God wanted them to write. If they had written only their own thoughts or ideas, it would have been impossible for the early prophets of the Old Testament to know the town where Jesus would be born or who His ancestors would be. The Bible foretold many events that only God could have known. There are actually over 300 prophecies about Jesus and His life in the Old Testament, and all of them were fulfilled.

Some of the New Testament writers personally witnessed the power of Jesus. They heard Him preach and saw Him perform miracles. They wrote about the things they saw and heard. Because God was in control of their writing, we can be sure that whatever is contained in the Bible is true and accurate. God tells us in Second Timothy 3:16-17, "All Scripture is God-breathed and is useful for teaching, rebuking, correcting and training in righteousness, so that the man of God may be thoroughly equipped for every good work." This means that we should read the Bible and then use its wisdom and principles to guide our lives. We can use the Bible as our standard to test everything that people tell us. For instance, some scientists say that humans were came about by chance as a result of evolution in nature. But the Bible tells us that God created the heavens and the earth and everything in them.

The Bible is our one true source that tells us how we can be saved—through faith in Jesus Christ (see Acts 16:31). Salvation comes through believing in Jesus Christ as God's only begotten Son, which means that we will go to Heaven to spend eternity with God—as opposed to spending eternity in hell with the devil. I can tell you from my own experiences—like the time that Jesus hugged me or during my near-death experience—that I am looking forward to eternal peace and joy. Having faith in God means that we believe what His Word, the Bible, tells us. If we truly believe in Him, we can't pick and choose what we want to believe in the Bible; after all, He was the editor.

Because the Bible can be complex in places, some people find it hard to accept. If a certain verse or sentence is taken out of context, it can be confusing. Very often, we need to understand the overall context of a Scripture passage or some background information to make sense of a verse. Asking the Holy Spirit to reveal meaning to us is a most important step to comprehending the depths of the Bible. Sometimes the Bible seems to be filled with paradoxes or contradictions. Themes of law and gospel, sin and grace, sinner and saint, slave and free, are found throughout the Bible. After thorough study, prayer, and insight from the Holy Spirit, we begin to see how these issues are balanced when considering the entirety of the Bible. The more time we spend reading the Bible, the more quickly the pieces will fit together. The Old Testament foretells the New Testament, and the New Testament fulfills the Old Testament. Scripture interprets Scripture when looked at in order and as a whole. We can be assured that God is consistent and that His Word is as well. If there is something that doesn't make sense to you when you read it, I encourage you to pray about it, and ask God for understanding.

Some Bibles have been translated using more modern language and therefore they are easier to understand. Unlike the King James Version that is filled with words such as "thou" and "proceedeth," recent versions are translated with today's reader in mind. A few of the more popular Holy Bible translations currently available include: the New International Version, the New King James Version, the New American Bible, the American Standard Version, the Revised Standard Version, The Message, the New Living Translation, and the Amplified Bible. The translation that you choose is a matter of personal choice, but you should be careful that you choose one that is entirely based on the original texts. Study Bibles are also available, which explain the Bible almost verse by verse. If you continue to struggle with a section, ask a Christian pastor, priest, or minister to explain it to you.

OTHER SOURCES OF INSPIRATION

Because God is so willing to reach us, He also uses other written materials based on the Bible to talk to us. These can include hymnals, daily devotionals, self-help or growth books, Bible study materials, magazines, or various other materials that contain principles found in Scripture. As long as the material is biblically based, God can use it to tell us things He wants us to know. The important thing is that the Scriptures are taken from an authentic translation of the Holy Bible. There are some "religions" that have their own translations of the Bible. These religions have altered the original manuscripts to fit their own doctrines or beliefs. These scriptures are not accurate and should not be used if you desire the truth.

Most Christians can tell you that, at some point in their walk with God, He used a certain verse, or hymn, or some other form of written Word to talk to them specifically. They may have read that same verse or sang that same song a hundred times before, but until God chose to convict their heart with His message, it didn't mean a thing to them. The story usually goes something like this: "While reading the verse, the words jumped out at me. It seems like God wrote this just for me, right now—the words were burned into my heart." At this point, the person completely and clearly understands exactly what the words mean and how they relate to him or her at that moment in time.

When God talks to people like this, their hearts and minds are convicted. They know without a doubt what God is saying to them. If this has ever happened to you, you know just what I'm talking about. Sometimes it could be an answer you've been waiting for, or maybe the word is a total surprise. Sometimes you hear something that you really wanted to hear; other times you'd rather not hear what He's telling you. Whatever the case, God can and will use His written Word to talk to people. And you can be sure that if He talks to you like this, He isn't wasting His breath—He expects a response. It could be a thank You, or it might be a change of heart or habit. It could be a certain task that He wants you to accomplish. The list of things that God can say to a person through Scripture and materials based on His Word is endless!

I have attended various Bible study groups at church and in people's homes. Each time I am involved in one of these groups, I have found that God uses these experiences to teach me something. Even though we have all read and studied the same material, it always amazes me that each person in the group walks away with something different at the end of the study—something uniquely for them. Because we are all at different stages in our walk with God, He customizes His Word for each of us. Just because a friend or neighbor may have a certain conviction after reading a passage in Ephesians doesn't mean that you will have that same revelation. Listen carefully to what God is saying to *you*.

OLD HABITS, NEW OPPORTUNITIES

Although I loved God with all my heart, I was still addicted to smoking pot back when I was working as a mechanic and had taken the manager's position. I was going to church regularly, reading the Bible, and praying daily, but I still had this stronghold of sin in my life. It was the dirty little secret that I kept hidden away. I had tried quitting and failed so many times that, by that point, I assumed I would never be set free from my addiction. The Lord used my new job to continue the sanctification process in me. I soon found out that I couldn't do my job as manager very well while still having drugs in my system. Although it was very difficult for me, this forced me to be sober during the work week, but I made up for it on the weekends.

One particular Friday morning, on my way to work, I was already starting to feel guilty for what I knew I was going to do that night. I was asking God for forgiveness and reciting some Bible verses that usually comforted me. I began singing the children's hymn "I am Jesus's Little Lamb," because it was the only one I had memorized. While I was singing, I started thinking about how good God had been to me in my life, even though I wasn't worthy of His love. All at once, I felt engulfed by His love, completely immersed from head to toe. I didn't see a light, like the time when He had hugged me as a child, but the experience was similar. At the time, I assumed that it was His way of showing me that He loved me, even though He knew I was going to smoke a joint that night. I now think He was trying to show me that I didn't need to smoke that night because His love was enough to comfort me. I wish I could say that I didn't smoke that night, but I did. The reason why I'm telling you this incident in this chapter is because of the verses and the hymn that I was reciting. I don't think I would have had this same encounter with God if I hadn't been meditating on His Word and singing a hymn to Him.

During this time in my life, I was enjoying a daily devotional along with my prayers almost every morning. I noticed that, on days when I didn't commit to morning prayer and devotion, everything seemed to fall apart. Because I took my job as manager seriously, I prayed for my department and my employees daily. On the days when I didn't read His Word and pray for my department, God proved to me over and over that we would have a lot more problems. On one particular day, I didn't take time for my morning prayers and devotions, and we had a horrible day at work. Everything went wrong. By the time I returned home that night, I was at the end of my rope—all I wanted was a little peace and quiet. Raising four children in a small house means that there is not much peace and quiet. Because I was already in a bad mood, it didn't take long before I lost my temper and started yelling at my family. In a short period of time, I caused almost my entire family to cry.

My wife told me it wasn't their fault I had had a bad day. The devil told me to go out to the garage and take a couple puffs of pot to relax. God told me to go pray and read my devotions that I had skipped that morning. I locked myself in our bedroom to pray and read. The day's devotion told a story about a man who had a bad day at work and came home yelling at his family. I read that sometimes the things we say in anger to other people get locked in their memory forever. God convicted my heart so strongly through that written message that even now, years later, it still brings tears to my eyes. I was crying so hard that I could barely talk, but I went back downstairs and gathered my family around the table. I read the short story to them, and then I apologized to them and asked them to forgive me. My kids remembered that day for a long time and would periodically bring it up.

RACING FEVER

As our family grew, I stopped ice-racing motorcycles in the winter but continued to participate in cross-country motorcycle races in the summer. I won numerous races in my class and even several state championships, but I never achieved an "overall A" class win at a race. Then one year, I finally won an "overall A" class trophy at the biggest and last race of the year. I didn't ride again that year, so by spring, I was really itching to ride. It was an early spring day, and the snow had just melted. My wife wanted me to do some painting inside the house, and I had told her I would, but I wanted to ride my motorcycle first. I had a small track behind my house that I practiced on. Because of my overall win at the last race, my head had swollen to gigantic proportions. It was pride. I wasn't bragging to anybody out loud, but God knew what was in my heart.

As I always did before I rode, I prayed for God to keep me safe. Remember my not-answered prayer list? Remember that I mentioned a prayer that God allowed the exact thing that I had prayed against to happen? Well, this is it. I took one slow lap around the track and realized that there was still ice under some of the dirt. I decided that it didn't matter because I was "good enough" to control the bike. I held the bike wide open and tried to ride the course as if it was the middle of summer. I never even made it around the track once. The bike came out from under me at about 65 miles per hour in a long sweeping corner. Because the type of racing that I was involved in was long-distance, it was common to crash and sometimes get hurt. I often would ride faster than I should, above my talent level, just to try to win. I raced once with a broken wrist and won my class. Another time, I crashed while riding, in the winter (without insurance), and had to give myself seven stitches when I got home. I learned that when you crash during a race, the best thing to do is to get back on the bike and try to ride it slowly until you can shake off the pain.

That day, my neighbor, who was a farmer, was out in his field spreading manure. I knew he was watching me when I began riding. After I crashed, I was able to get the clutch pulled in so that the engine didn't stall. I stood the bike up and saw that my neighbor was standing up on his tractor so that he could see me. My pride and stupidity told me to get back on the bike and try to shake it off. I did, and soon realized, as I was trying to turn the bike for the corners, that I couldn't use my left arm at all. I was only idling along—and the pain was incredible.

My practice track was next to the railroad tracks, and I decided that I would ride on the access road beside the railroad tracks so I wouldn't have to try to turn the bike. I rode down the access road for about a quarter of a mile, hoping to shake off the pain, but it wasn't working. I decided to turn around and go home. When I tried to turn the bike around, I rode into a small tree because I couldn't steer the bike. The tree had very long thorns, and one of the thorns went through my leather riding glove and through the end of the index finger on my left hand. This time the motorcycle quit, and I just sat there. I have never claimed to be smart, and I guess this story proves it. My pride had hurt me not only once, but twice that day. I was able to pull the thorn out of my finger with my teeth. I got the bike started and rode it home. My wife was not happy.

I decided that, if I could get over the pain, I would be OK, and I wouldn't have to go to the hospital. I had some morphine patches that someone had given me a long time ago, and I decided that now was the time to use them. I medicated myself all weekend and finally gave in and went to the doctor on Monday morning. The doctor couldn't believe that I had hurt myself that badly on Saturday but hadn't come in until Monday. I had completely torn the rotator cuff away from my shoulder; only the muscles and tendons held my arm in place. The doctor performed surgery and reattached the rotator cuff. Because of the severity of the injury, I had to take a lot of time off work. I am a very active person, and being unable to work or use my arm was hard for me. One day, when I was sitting at home feeling crabby over the whole situation, my shoulder really started to hurt. It felt like someone was pinching it in a vice.

My wife decided to make my favorite meal that night. Anyone who knows me can tell you that I enjoy eating. When it comes right down to it, I *love* to eat. When my wife put the steak and shrimp on the table, my shoulder began to hurt even worse. I was hungry, and I wanted to eat, but instead I went to our room to lie down. I saw my Bible on the nightstand and decided to read a little. I opened it to a random page, and the words cut right to my heart. It said that God loves us but that when we sin we still have to suffer the consequences for our sin. I instantly knew that it was no coincidence that these were the first words that I read. I prayed to God and told Him that I was sorry for my foolish pride. I also told Him that I was sorry for getting crabby over the situation—it was my own fault. God is a loving God who wants to treat us as a loving father would. As soon as I acknowledged my sin to Him, He instantly took the pain away, and I even ate my supper before it got cold. Praise God for His mercy! God wants to talk to us through His Word, but sometimes it takes pain in our lives before we are ready to listen.

COINCIDENCES

One day when I was at work, a coworker told me about his belief in reincarnation. That same morning, only hours earlier, I had read a devotion and Bible verses about that exact subject. I told this man that I didn't believe in coincidences and I thought God was using this situation to try to talk to him. He said that he wasn't calling me a liar but that he wanted me to bring the material in so he could see for himself. I tore out that day's devotion when I got home and took it to work the next day. I explained to him that the Bible verses listed at the top of the page supported the content of the devotion and that he should look up those verses and read them first. After I handed him the torn-out page, he started reading it. I realized that he was reading the wrong side of the paper; that page was actually from two days ago. I was starting to interrupt him when I saw the heading from that day's devotion. The heading read, "Build up treasure in heaven, not on earth where moth and rust can destroy." His face looked troubled as he was reading it. You see, this man was very rich and had spent most of his life trying to secure his fortune. I don't know if he took to heart what he read, but I can tell you that I fully believe God was trying to talk to him, trying to reach out to him through His written Word.

I once read a short story written by a pastor about something he had witnessed. Although I don't remember some of the specifics, I remember the point of the story. He was teaching a confirmation class, and one of his students had a bad attitude. He asked the young man what the problem was, and the pupil said that the Bible was too hard to understand. The pastor told him that he didn't believe that was true and that he could prove it. He told the young man to open the Bible to anywhere he wanted and to start reading and then the class would decide if they could understand it or not. The pupil opened the Bible and started reading. The pastor wrote that the young man's voice dropped almost to a whisper. The words he read were, "Only a fool believes in his heart that there is no God." Apparently the young man's problem wasn't that he couldn't *understand* the Bible but that he didn't *believe* the Bible. God can talk to us through His Word, but if we don't listen to it or believe it, that's our choice.

I have a very similar story. In fact, my story actually happened shortly after I read that one. I was driving down the road one day when the Little Whisper of the Holy Spirit told me to call a customer whom I hadn't heard from for quite a while. I argued with the notion, but I finally gave in and called the man. I asked him about the last truck I had worked on for him, and he said that the truck was fine but that he had been having a few problems. His best friend had been shot and killed. He was really having a hard time dealing with the pain, so he got drunk and went to the cemetery where his friend was buried. The police found him there with his hunting rifle and some beer. They committed him to the local mental hospital for observation. Although he had been released, he wasn't back to work yet. I knew that he had a drinking problem before this happened, and it sounded like this incident made it worse.

We talked for over an hour that day, and I told him that God would work it all out. He told me he was angry at God for allowing his friend to be killed and said that if God really were a loving God, none of this would have happened. I remembered the story from the pastor about his pupil, and I told this man to pray to God for guidance, to ask God to speak to him, and then to read his Bible. I told him to open it up wherever he wanted and to start reading. After we got off the phone, I prayed for him. I prayed that God would answer his prayer and that He would talk to him through His Word. I waited a week before I called the man back and asked what had happened. He said that God had not talked to him and that he was still having a rough time. I was shocked; I felt in my heart that I had told the man exactly what God wanted me to say. I was sure that God would answer his prayer. I asked him what he had read when he opened up the Bible. He said that the first words he read were that we should trust God with our whole heart. Then he slammed the Bible shut and decided that God wasn't listening to him.

I instantly thanked God for answering my prayer. I told the man that God had answered his prayer and that He was telling him the exact thing that he needed to hear. I told him that I was sorry that he couldn't see that God was talking to him, but it seemed very obvious to me that He was. Sometimes God tells us things that we don't want to hear or things that we don't want to believe. Just like in this case, we might be so close to the problem that we can't see it. When this happens, it doesn't mean that God isn't talking to us but that we aren't listening to God.

Through these various stories, I hope it is obvious to you that God can and will talk to people (everyday people like you and me) through His written Word. God truly does love us and wants a relationship with us. Just like any other relationship, it takes effort from both parties to have open communication. Jesus tells us in John 6:45-50:

> *It is written in the Prophets: "They will all be taught by God." Everyone who listens to the Father and learns from Him comes to Me. No one has seen the Father except the One who is from God; only He has seen the Father. I tell you the truth, he who believes has everlasting life. I am the*

bread of life. Your forefathers ate the manna in the desert, yet they died. But here is the bread that comes down from heaven, which a man may eat and not die.

YOUR TURN

Write about the times when God talked to you through the Bible. Write about the times when God talked to you through other written words that were based on Scripture.

_____

_____

_____

_____

_____

_____

_____

_____

_____

_____

_____

_____

_____

_____

_____

STUDY QUESTIONS

1. What does Second Timothy 3:16-17 tell us about how we should use the Bible?

2. In Hebrews 4:12, what does "living and active" mean?

3. The protestant Bible is made up of sixty-six books, thirty-nine Old Testament books and twenty-seven New Testament books—with a four-hundred-year gap between. The Catholic Bible has an extra seven books, called the Deuterocanonical books (also known as the Apocrypha). What Scripture did the Jews in Jesus's day have?

4. Who is the author and editor of the Bible? What does Second Peter 1:19-21 tell us about the more than three hundred biblical prophecies about Jesus that have been fulfilled?

5. Are there contradictions in the Bible? (See Deuteronomy 29:29; and First Corinthians 13:9-12.) What is the best way to handle complex or confusing passages?

6. What does the phrase *other written Word* refer to?

7. Are you a Berean? (See Acts 17:11.)

JOURNAL

CHAPTER 4

GOD TALKS THROUGH THE SPOKEN WORD

THE BIBLE TELLS US IN HEBREWS 4:12, "FOR THE WORD OF God is living and active. Sharper than any double-edged sword, it penetrates even to dividing soul and spirit, joints and marrow; it judges the thoughts and attitudes of the heart." For these very reasons, God uses His spoken Word to talk to us, through whomever He chooses. His spoken Word can be heard on a radio or television. His Word can be shared through a parent or a friend. He can use a neighbor or even a stranger to talk to you. Because God and His Word are living and active, there are no barriers to keep us from hearing Him talk to us. He can just as easily use a common everyday sinner to speak through as He can use the pastor in the church down the street. The power is in His message, not in the messenger!

Because all humans are sinful and not perfect, God's human messengers are not perfect. There are many stories in the Bible that prove this point. God chose Noah to rebuild the land after the great flood—but after Noah planted a vineyard, he got drunk (see Gen. 9:20-21). God used Moses to set the nation of Israel free; but Moses also committed murder (see Exod. 2:14). God used Rahab to hide two men who were sent to spy on the promised land; she was a prostitute (see Josh. 2:1). We are told that David was a man after God's own heart (see Acts 13:22), but we also read in the Bible that he had an adulterous affair and had the woman's husband killed (see 2 Sam. 11). These stories begin in the Old Testament and continue throughout the Bible. God uses everyday men and women to accomplish His plans.

In First Corinthians 1:26-29, the apostle Paul talked about this very subject. He said:

> *Brothers, think of what you were when you were called. Not many of you were wise by human standards; not many were influential; not many were of noble birth. But God chose the foolish things of the world to shame the wise; God chose the weak things of the world to shame the strong. He chose the lowly things of this world and the despised things—and the things that are not— to nullify the things that are, so that no one may boast before him.*

Right now, in our world, we hear stories about pastors, priests, ministers, and evangelists who get into trouble and make bad decisions. In light of everything that we read in the Bible, this should not surprise us. We are human, and we make mistakes. On one hand, these stories could sadden us because of our human condition, but on the other hand, they should make us happy to know that God loves us anyway. Jesus tells us in John 3:16, "For God so loved the world that He gave His one and only Son, that whoever believes in Him shall not perish but have eternal life." We are also told in Romans 5:8, "But God demonstrates His own love for us in this: While we were still sinners, Christ died for us."

DISCERNMENT

God can, will, and does speak to us through fellow sinners. But because there are so many different religions, ideas, and points of view, it can sometimes be tricky to decide if what we are being told is truly from God. If someone is going to be bold enough to try to preach to someone else, they probably believe what they are saying, or at least they feel strongly about it. The Bible tells us very clearly that it is our job to decide if what we are being told is from God or not. The good news is that Scriptures show us how to make this decision. First John 4:1-3 tells us:

> *Dear friends, do not believe every spirit, but test the spirits to see whether they are from God, because many false prophets have gone out into the world. This is how you can recognize the Spirit of God: Every spirit that acknowledges that Jesus Christ has come in the flesh is from God, but every spirit that does not acknowledge Jesus is not from God. This is the spirit of the antichrist, which you have heard is coming and even now is already in the world.*

As the old saying goes, don't believe everything you are told. The more we read the Bible and become familiar with God's Word, the easier it becomes to "test the spirits." There are many people in the world claiming to spread a message from God, and some truly are. But there are others who may sound and look like a messenger from God, but in reality, they are peddling the devil's message. We must weigh everything we hear against what the Bible says, and we must lift our hearts in prayer to have the truth revealed to us. We can't make judgments based on our own wisdom or thoughts. We can't make judgments based on how old, how young, or how religious we think the person is who is telling us something. God is faithful to us, and He will lead and guide us to the truth when we seek it. The Bible

tells us in Acts 17:11, "Now the Bereans were of more noble character than the Thessalonians, for they received the message with great
eagerness and examined the Scriptures every day to see if what Paul
said was true." Let us be like the Bereans and use our Bibles as the
standard that we measure everything else against.

EVERYDAY PEOPLE'S WORDS

I am constantly amazed that God uses me, an everyday sinner, to
talk to people. People like Bob and Joe. I am humbled—not boast-
ful—that God has chosen me to deliver His messages to others. He
uses everyday people to tell others about Himself. Are you listening
for His voice? Do you have a message for someone who needs to hear
from God?

Sometime after we had moved back to our hometown, I heard
that the teenage daughter of a lady I used to work with had run away
from home. I called her and told her that I would pray for her family.
Weeks later, after I had finished my morning prayers, I felt that God
wanted me to call her and tell her to trust Him that everything would
be all right. She thanked me but said that she was losing hope because
no one had heard from the girl. Hours later, that same day, many
states away, the police found her daughter alive and healthy. I know
in my heart that God had me call her that morning with that message
so that, when her daughter was found in the afternoon, she would
know that God is real and she could trust Him. Praise God!

One Sunday morning, while my family and I were getting
ready to go to church, I felt that God was telling me to pray about
something in particular. We had been invited to a birthday party for
the daughter of a woman who was living with one of my long-time
friends. My wife and I had already decided that our family was not
going to go because we were not sure if the atmosphere would be
appropriate for our small children. While my wife and I stood in the

bathroom getting ready for church, I told her that God was telling me to pray right then and there. We held hands and started to pray for the girl and her family situation.

The pastor's message that morning cut right to our hearts. He challenged the congregation to pick out someone they knew was not a believer and to pray for them. He said that after we prayed, we had to be willing to let God use us to help that person, if God so chose. Tears were streaming down my face as I listened to the pastor's words from God. After church, we talked about it and decided that it was obvious that God wanted us to go to the birthday party as a family and to be part of His plan. On the way, we stopped and bought a few Christian books that were written for girls her age. Although our children were much younger, they played with the birthday girl the entire time we were there. We found that God had two goals that day; one was for us to give the girl some encouraging Christian material, and the other was to have our children there for the girl to play with. There were no other children or friends at the party, just adults and a sibling. As we were leaving, the girl thanked us repeatedly for coming and bringing our kids. We were very glad that we ended up going to the party, for the girl's sake and for ours. We were glad we obeyed God's leading. As the Bible tells us in James 1:22-25:

Do not merely listen to the word, and so deceive yourselves. Do what it says. Anyone who listens to the word but does not do what it says is like a man who looks at his face in a mirror and, after looking at himself, goes away and immediately forgets what he looks like. But the man who looks intently into the perfect law that gives freedom, and continues to do this, not forgetting what he has heard, but doing it—he will be blessed in what he does.

During my lifetime, God has talked to me through several different people, and I thank God for every one of them. In His great wisdom, God decided to use everyday people to tell others about Himself and His love. This way, He can show non-believers that being a Christian doesn't mean that you are perfect, but that you are forgiven. Again, the power is in His message, not in the messenger! The Bible says in Second Corinthians 4:7, "But we have this treasure in jars of clay to show that this all-surpassing power is from God and not from us." It has been my experience that God will use somebody to talk to us at just the right time, exactly when we need to hear it the most. What a blessing it can be when God gives us His valuable Word and we listen to it. Proverbs 25:11-12 says, "A word aptly spoken is like apples of gold in settings of silver. Like an earring of gold or an ornament of fine gold is a wise man's rebuke to a listening ear."

HIS POWERFUL WORD

God's Word is very powerful. When Jesus was being tempted by the devil in the desert, He answered all three of the devil's temptations with God's own Word (see Matt. 4:1-11). This story shows us the importance of knowing God's Word and helps us to appreciate the effectiveness of using it. The Bible also tells us that Jesus is the perfect example to follow as a model for our lives. A passage from the Bible that makes this point rather clearly is found in Colossians 3:16-17:

> *Let the word of Christ dwell in you richly as you teach and admonish one another with all wisdom, and as you sing psalms, hymns and spiritual songs with gratitude in your hearts to God. And whatever you do, whether in word or deed, do it all in the name of the Lord Jesus, giving thanks to God the Father through Him.*

Another passage that adds to that point is Second Timothy 3:16-17, which says, "All Scripture is God-breathed and is useful for teaching, rebuking, correcting and training in righteousness, so that the man of God may be thoroughly equipped for every good work."

I told you earlier about my first prayer as a child, when I prayed to Jesus to give me a hug and He instantly responded. I said that prayer because of the Sunday school teacher who told me the story about Jesus loving little children. This man changed my life forever by sharing one story from God's Word with me. I urge you to think about that for a moment. I would guess that, if you are reading this book, you may be a Christian. If so, I plead with you to share God's Word with everyone, every chance you have. If you are not a Christian, I plead with you to be open to God's voice, to take the chance and find out for yourself how good God is. Start by reading the Bible—God's Word is powerful. The New Testament is filled with stories about how Jesus is the best friend you'll ever have. He will never leave you—He is always by your side, loving you through your everyday life.

SPEAKING TO YOU

Another time when God spoke His Word to me through someone else was just after Lori and I were married. I had been at a school out of town and was traveling home. As I was driving along in the rental car, I was praying to God to help me turn my life around and be a better person. Thoughts began to pop into my head that I realized were not my own. Let me stop here and dwell on that idea for a moment. If someone says that a thought popped into his mind, what does that really mean? What does that sound like? Is it accurate to say that a thought is something your mind hears? Think about the illustration of that old cartoon, the one with an angel on one shoulder and a devil on the other—now this idea makes more sense. The thoughts that come to our minds most often are our own, but they can be from God—or from the devil.

The thoughts I was having while driving home, the quiet Whisper in my head, kept telling me that I couldn't change without the help of the Holy Spirit. I kept hearing that, unless I completely surrendered my heart to God, my nature would be fighting against the Holy Spirit. After a while, I stopped praying and decided to turn on the car radio. "Coincidently," the radio was tuned to a religious station and a sermon was just beginning—the focus of the message was submitting to the Holy Spirit so He can change your life. I couldn't believe what I was hearing. Some of the exact statements and phrases that were being said by this pastor had just been popping into my mind. It was very obvious to me that God was using this pastor to confirm His Word to me. (Often we find that the Lord will repeat Himself to us.) This also proved to me that the thoughts I was having were not my own but that they were from God. (This story also fits in with Chapter 4, on the Holy Spirit, because surely it was the Holy Spirit whispering His thoughts to me.)

Earlier in the book, I told you about my wife's mother being ill and how we prayed to God for an answer about moving back to our hometown. I saved part of the story for this chapter. What I didn't tell you earlier was that, at that same time, I was offered an attractive managerial position in another part of the state. I decided to check out the place before making a decision; so I spent the weekend there. On Saturday morning, I read the Bible and spent time in prayer. I left the motel, planning to give the town a once-over and then ask people questions about the area. I drove from one end of the town to the other. It looked clean and pretty healthy. I pulled into a gas station to turn around, and an elderly man was walking out of the station.

The Little Whisper told me that I should ask this man about the town. I rolled down my window, introduced myself, and told him about my job offer. He told me that he had lived in the area his whole life and that it was a nice friendly town. The next things he said spoke directly to my heart. He went on to say that, if I put God first in my life, everything else would fall into place. He said that family came right after God and that work was third in line. He told me that, when he was young and first married, he went to church to make his wife happy. One Sunday, the priest preached on the importance of tithing. When they got home, his wife made it clear that she thought they should start tithing. He tried to argue with her, but her mind was made up, so he gave in. They decided that night to give God the first 10 percent of his wages.

He was working in a lumberyard back then, and the next day, he was called into the office. The boss told him that they liked his work ethic and that they wanted to see him stick around, so they were going to give him a raise. The raise made up for the 10 percent they had decided to give God, plus it gave him a two-cent raise. He reminded me that just the two-cent raise alone, above the 10 percent, was a good raise in those days. He said that right then and there he knew that this God that his wife believed in was a real God, a living God. He went on to say that he had worked at that place for many years and then started his own business with a small investment. He had recently retired and sold that business to his kids for a large sum of money.

This man had no way of knowing what was going on in my life, or the questions that I was struggling with. Toward the end of our conversation, he asked me why I had stopped and asked him about the town. I told him that God obviously had directed me to him. As I drove away from the gas station, I knew exactly what God wanted me to do. God had the man address every single subject that I needed to look at in order to help me make the decisions I was facing. His advice answered the important questions I had, ones that I hadn't even asked him. God used this man and his testimony to speak to me, a stranger at a gas station. Praise God for using everyday people to tell other everyday people His Word.

TRAGEDY AND TRIUMPH

When—not if—tragedy strikes our lives, we can hold on to what God tells us in Romans 8:28. "And we know that in all things God works for the good of those who love Him...." Very often, we have a hard time seeing how any good can come out of a tragedy, but we have to remember that we don't see the big picture that God sees. We also need to remember that we can believe all of the beautiful promises that God makes to us. If you have had something happen to you that you are having a hard time getting over, I urge you to find someone you can talk to who has been through a similar experience. God can use someone else's past pain to help you through your current pain. Or maybe you know someone who is dealing with an issue that you yourself have encountered. Your advice and support to that person could be invaluable. Let me encourage you to share your past victories, failures, and struggles. I have found that honesty, although not always pretty, is a powerful tool in setting people free.

Let me say that I spent most of my life as a mechanic by trade, a sinner by nature. Never in a million years did I ever consider writing a book—much less a book about God. But God used several people to tell me that I had to share these stories. The last person God used was the one who pushed me over the edge. I was sharing some "God-stories" with her, and while I was talking, she stopped me and said that God had told her six times in the last 15 minutes that I had to put these stories into book form. If it hadn't been for all of the other people who had told me this first, I probably wouldn't have listened. Once again, God used everyday people to accomplish His work.

I hope that, after reading this chapter and these examples, it is clear to you that God can and will use other everyday people to talk to you. The Bible is full of stories about God using people to accomplish His plans for us. I also hope that you will see how important it is to allow God to use you to talk to others. The Bible tells us that, as believers, we are all part of the Body of Christ, and although each part is different, each part is very important to the whole (see 1 Cor. 12:12-27). You are important to God because He has certain things that only you can accomplish for Him. He has placed each of us in different positions, and therefore, we each have unique opportunities to share His words with others. The Bible tells us in Ephesians 2:10, "For we are God's workmanship, created in Christ Jesus to do good works, which God prepared in advance for us to do." How exciting it is to think that God has specific plans in mind for each of us!

YOUR TURN

Write about the times when God spoke to you through other people. It may have been a comment that lifted you up or advice that gave you guidance or direction. It could have been a time when you were warned or rebuked. Maybe you listened, or maybe you wish you would have—either way you can see now that it was from God.

_____

_____

_____

_____

_____

_____

_____

_____

_____

_____

_____

_____

_____

_____

STUDY QUESTIONS

1. When it comes to hearing God through other people, is the power in the message or in the messenger? (See Hebrews 4:12; Second Corinthians 4:7; and Proverbs 25:11-12.)

2. List as many sources as you can think of that God could use to speak to you. Who couldn't He use? Why? Are you sure?

3. Does God only use perfect people to speak for Him? Were the heroes of the Bible perfect? (See Romans 3:23; and First Corinthians 1:26-29.) Why is this important to understand?

4. The Bible tells us not to believe everything we are told, but to test it first (see First John 4:1-3; Acts 17:11; Col. 3:16-17).

How do we go about testing what we hear and developing discernment?

5. According to First Kings 13:1-22, what consequences may we face if we don't listen and discern well?

6. In what ways does God want to use you? (See Ephesians 2:10; and First Corinthians 12:12-27.) How does God empower you to do His work? (See Ephesians 3:20; Acts 1:8.)

7. Who is God calling you to reach out to in His name?

JOURNAL

CHAPTER 5

GOD TALKS THROUGH THE HOLY SPIRIT

THE BIBLE TELLS US THAT, AFTER JESUS HAD BEEN CRUCIFIED and was buried, He rose again three days later. (See Mark 15–16.) After Jesus rose from the dead, for 40 days He appeared to many people on many separate occasions. During one of the last times that He appeared to His disciples, He spoke to them the "Great Commission." He gave His followers our marching orders. Matthew records the event in chapter 28:

> *Then Jesus came to them and said, "All authority in heaven and on earth has been given to Me. Therefore go and make disciples of all nations, baptizing them in the name of the Father and of the Son and of the Holy Spirit, and teaching them to obey everything I have commanded you. And surely I am with you always, to the very end of the age"* (Matthew 28:18-20).

Having this Scripture as a solid foundation is a good place to start Chapter 5 because it helps us to realize what is important to

Jesus. Jesus told us that we are to baptize people in the name of the Father and of the Son and of the Holy Spirit. Jesus was showing us the threefold nature of God. Although the word *trinity* is not used in Scripture, this picture of a triune God is found throughout the Bible. (See Mark 1:9-11; Acts 1:4-5; Romans 5:5-6; and Matthew 28:19.) He is one God made up of three persons, Father, Son, and Holy Spirit.

Jesus also told us that He would be with us always. He only appeared to the disciples one more time before He was taken up into Heaven. Let's think about this for a moment. Jesus told His disciples that He would be with them always, and then He ascended out of sight and into Heaven—not to be seen physically by them again. As confusing and contradictory as this might sound to us, can you imagine what His disciples would have been thinking? Before Jesus died, He told them what would happen after His death. He said:

> *If you love Me, you will obey what I command. And I will ask the Father, and He will give you another Counselor to be with you forever—the Spirit of truth. The world cannot accept Him, because it neither sees Him nor knows Him. But you know Him, for He lives with you and will be in you. I will not leave you as orphans; I will come to you. Before long, the world will not see Me anymore, but you will see Me. Because I live, you also will live* (John 14:15-19).

Jesus also said:

> *All this I have spoken while still with you. But the Counselor, the Holy Spirit, whom the Father will send in My name, will teach you all things and will remind you of everything I have said to you. Peace I leave with you; My peace I give you. I do not give to you as the world gives. Do not let your hearts be troubled and do not be afraid* (John 14:25-27).

Jesus told them more about the Holy Spirit in John 16:

> *But I tell you the truth: It is for your good that I am going away. Unless I go away, the Counselor will not come to you; but if I go, I will send Him to you....But when He, the Spirit of truth, comes, He will guide you into all truth...* (John 16:7,13).

Ten days after Jesus ascended into Heaven, He sent the Holy Spirit to His followers. The Bible calls this event "Pentecost." Acts 2 gives an account of what happened in Jerusalem. There was a sound like that of a strong wind, and people saw what looked like tongues of fire rest on each of the believers. As the Holy Spirit filled the people, they spoke in foreign languages. At the same time, there was a large religious festival taking place, called the Feast of Weeks. Because of this festival in the city, Jews from all over the known world were there. As the local, Spirit-filled followers of Jesus began speaking about God in a variety of different languages, the Bible says that a crowd gathered in amazement because they each heard the disciples preaching in their own native tongue. As the crowd listened, they were cut to the heart and asked what they could do to be saved. Peter told them to repent and be baptized, and then they too would receive the gift of the Holy Spirit. The Bible says that about 3,000 people became believers in Jesus and were baptized that day. God timed Pentecost so that His message of good news would be heard by an international audience. The people returned to their countries and shared the message of Jesus.

HIS GIFT TO US

Jesus continues to offer the gift of the Holy Spirit to everyday people every day. Have you accepted His offer? Paul wrote in Ephesians 1:13-14:

And you also were included in Christ when you heard the word of truth, the gospel of your salvation. Having believed, you were marked in Him with a seal, the promised Holy Spirit, who is a deposit guaranteeing our inheritance until the redemption of those who are God's possession—to the praise of His glory.

In short, we hear, we believe, and we receive. Jesus promised that, after He left, He would send the Holy Spirit, and He did. He said that the Holy Spirit would teach us, remind us of what He taught, and guide us. We can see from the story of Pentecost that this Spirit did all of these things. The Holy Spirit told the disciples what to say and how to say it, and He helped them to say it with power. The Spirit continued to communicate or talk to the disciples and Jesus's followers. God still uses the Holy Spirit to talk to us today.

Jesus told His disciples, "But you will receive power when the Holy Spirit comes on you; and you will be My witnesses in Jerusalem, and in all Judea and Samaria, and to the ends of the earth" (Acts 1:8). This power came in many different forms. The disciples were given courage and peace. They were able to heal the sick and the lame, and even to drive demons out of people. So what should we expect from the Holy Spirit? What will He do for us, and how will He help us? In John chapters 14, 15, and 16, He is called a Comforter, Counselor, or a Helper, depending on the translation. When we think of the word *comfort,* we usually think of sympathy or compassion, but the Holy Spirit actually gives us staying power, the courage and the direction to get through trials and circumstances. When we pray to God for help, we should look for strength rather than sympathy from the Holy Spirit. He doesn't just pat us on the back and tell us that everything will be OK. He empowers us to get through our problems—I know from experience.

I told you earlier about the great dog with the broken tail that God gave us early in our marriage. We had Eve for nine years before she got sick and died unexpectedly. She had slept in our bed with us and went almost everywhere we did. She was part of the family, and when she died, we were crushed. A few days after she died, I came home from work and went into the backyard where we buried her and began to cry. I was praying to God for comfort, but as I remember now, I was actually having a pity party for myself. After 15 or 20 minutes of prayer, I heard the Holy Spirit whisper "enough." He then told me to listen because He was going to tell me what to say when I had to speak in front of the church in a few months. I was part of a newly-formed committee at church and had missed the first meeting. But someone called to say that I would be making an announcement in front of the church regarding an upcoming stewardship program. There was a small book I needed to read, but the supply was gone, and they had to order more. The caller told me not to worry about what to say because the book was very detailed and there were still a few months before I had to speak.

As the Holy Spirit told me what He wanted me to say, I realized that I should be writing it down so I wouldn't forget. I ran into the house and grabbed a pen and notebook. My wife could see that I had been crying, and because of the way I ran into the house, she asked me what in the world was going on. I answered that I would tell her later and ran back outside. I wrote down six pages in that small pocket notebook. When I received the stewardship book weeks later, I compared it to what the Holy Spirit had told me and found that nothing was missing. In fact, the Holy Spirit had actually given me some extra material that turned out to be very powerful for the congregation. This was clearly a time where God gave me strength and direction more than sympathy and compassion, especially since I had never spoken in front of a large group and was very nervous about it. After the Holy Spirit had finished talking to me, I was no longer focusing on myself or on my sorrow, but I was thinking about what God wanted me to do. I felt better because He redirected my thoughts away from myself and toward Him.

Another time that God used this same tactic was when my work truck had broken down, and I was working on it in my garage at the house. A long-time friend stopped by to see how it was going. While he was there, he asked if I wanted to smoke a little pot with him, and I agreed. Before he left, he took another small chunk of pot out of his bag and laid it on my workbench. I told him that I didn't want it, but he insisted. After he left, I took the small chunk into the house and flushed it down the toilet because I had promised God that I would try not to use or own illegal substances. I was standing inside the house asking God for forgiveness and telling Him I was sorry. I was crying and feeling pretty crappy inside as I was praying. The Holy Spirit whispered again and told me "enough." He told me to open my eyes and look up. I was facing the end of our main room in the house. The Holy Spirit told me to build a large cross and put it in that spot—the place where I had intended to put an idol—a head mount of a trophy buck.

I immediately got on the phone to find black walnut boards out of which to make a cross. The local lumberyards didn't stock them but "coincidentally" a man who worked at one of the lumberyards had exactly the right size boards at his house, and he sold them to me for a fraction of their worth. Before I realized it, I was no longer depressed about my truck breaking down or about breaking my promise to God about smoking pot. I received the forgiveness that God offers and the strength and stamina that He is so willing to give us.

These last two examples of the Holy Spirit communicating show us something that many people have found to be true. Often when God speaks to us through the Holy Spirit, He interrupts our current train of thought—He breaks in and says, "Listen up!" Then He drops something into our minds that is new and refreshing and God-focused.

People might describe this as a spontaneous thought. Many times we find that it is something we never would have thought of or even could have thought of on our own.

LISTENING FOR HIM

God talks to us through an inner whisper or audible voice. This whisper or voice is the Holy Spirit. While writing this book, it has become very obvious to me that this inner whisper is one of the most common ways in which He talks to me. A lot of Christians would refer to this guiding as their God-given conscience. To many mature believers, listening to this inner voice becomes "second nature," a routine part of their daily walk.

Sometimes when sharing my personal stories about God and how He talks to me, fellow Christians tell me their own stories about how they hear God speak. Sharing stories with other believers is encouraging for all who hear them. It gives concrete evidence to the fact that God talks to people. There have been times when I have heard the Holy Spirit whisper while in a group of other believers, and when I tell the group what I heard, someone else in the group almost always says that they heard the same thing. This can be very exciting! This validates and confirms what God said.

But sometimes when sharing these stories, the opposite happens. The other person might say, "You're crazy if you think you can hear God talking to you," or, "That's impossible." The comment that bothers me most, though, is when someone says that I'm lucky that God talks to me, because God doesn't talk to them. My friend Tim, a member of my church, used to say this to me. He said that, although he had been a Christian for years, God had never talked to him. God has since shown us both that God had been talking to him, but Tim hadn't realized it. As I share Tim's story, I hope you will realize that God has been talking to you too!

ACCOUNTABILITY

I had struggled with drug addiction for many years. Because Tim is my friend, he wanted to help me break the habit. One of our pastors told us that he has an accountability partner who helps him when he is struggling with problems. Tim offered to be my accountability partner. I agreed, but we didn't know exactly what that would mean or how it would work. A few weeks after our agreement, I was at a friend's house, and he had just lit a pot pipe. He was about to hand it to me when my cell phone rang. It was Tim calling to see how I was doing. I told him I was fine, and we small-talked for a few minutes. Although I felt a little funny, I didn't really give his call a second thought at the time.

Another week or so passed, and once again, I was somewhere I shouldn't have been. Another friend was just about to hand me a burning joint when my cell phone rang. I looked at the caller identification and saw that it was Tim. I answered the phone and talked to him briefly. But I got off the phone as quickly as I could because I felt convicted inside. I tried not to think about it and smoked anyway. I reasoned to myself that I no longer had drugs of my own and that I wasn't smoking every day like I used to.

A few more weeks passed, and after I had just finished working on a Saturday afternoon, I stopped at a friend's garage. We smoked the little bit of pot that he had left. He told me that if I hung out for a little while, it would be worth my time because somebody was going to drop off some really good stuff. I had told my wife and kids that I would try to get home early that day so that we could do something together. As we sat there waiting, my phone rang. I looked at the number and saw that it was Tim. I was so convicted that it felt as if God Himself was calling me. Now I realized that these calls were not coincidences, and I couldn't even answer the phone. My mind was spinning as I thought about what had just happened—again. I told my friend I couldn't stay, and I went straight home to my family.

The next day, we went to church and Sunday school like always. I avoided Tim that day and just kept thinking about everything that had happened over the past couple of months. I knew without a doubt that Tim was hearing God talk to him but that he just didn't realize or discern it. There was absolutely no other way to explain him calling three times at the exact moment before I was about to smoke pot. I also knew how badly Tim wanted to hear the voice of God. This put me in the predicament of either telling Tim the truth, or protecting my pride and avoiding shame by not admitting what was happening.

That Monday I finally gave in to God and made the right decision. I called Tim and asked him why he called me on Saturday. He said that he had actually been taking a little nap, and he woke up with me on his mind and felt compelled to call me. I asked why he had called me on the two previous occasions, and again he said that I had just popped into his mind and thought he should call me. I told Tim the truth about what had been going on each time he called me. It was obvious that he was reacting to a prompting by the Holy Spirit.

After we discussed it awhile, Tim realized that he was hearing God speak to him, but it wasn't how he had expected. He had the notion that, when God spoke to someone, it had to be dramatic or spectacular, that it would be unmistakable. I have found that this is exactly what most people think, but this it is usually not the case.

For many people, when God talks to them through the whisper of the Holy Spirit, they describe it as a thought that pops into their minds. It sometimes might also be described as an urge or a prompting without any forethought. As mentioned previously, the Holy Spirit often interrupts our thoughts with a new focus. Some may try to reason these thoughts away, but other times it is impossible to make any correlation between a Holy Spirit whisper and anything else going on in our minds. The thoughts we have only come from three sources: God, the devil, and ourselves. (Remember the cartoon we talked about?) Since birth, we have been receiving thoughts and ideas without realizing it. That is why these different ranges of thoughts seem so natural, and we often have a hard time discerning their true origins.

HIS VOICE

As we acquire more discernment, it becomes easier to recognize the source of our thoughts. As we grow closer to the Lord and spend more time with Him, we begin to recognize His voice more clearly. Jesus tells us, "My sheep listen to My voice; I know them, and they follow Me" (John 10:27). When we have a thought that comes into our mind from God, it will always be in line with the truths that we find in the Bible. If we have some type of "bad" thought, we can be sure that it either came from our sinful nature or from an evil source. We find that when the devil was trying to tempt Jesus into sinning in the desert, he quoted Scripture to Jesus. Satan took passages out of context and twisted their true meaning. (See Matthew 4:1-11.) The devil continues to use this tactic with Christians today!

God gave us the Old Testament law first and then the New Testament gospel. If we are about to sin, the Holy Spirit will tell us that it is wrong (law) and that we should not do it. After we sin, He will tell us to repent, and then He will offer us complete forgiveness (gospel). The devil also uses these terms, but he does it backward from God's way. Before we sin, he tells us that it's OK because God will forgive us, but after we sin, satan tells us that we are worthless sinners who can't or shouldn't be forgiven. He might even quote Scripture to us like he did to Jesus, but it will always be used in an inappropriate way. He will use the gospel to entice us to sin, and he will use the law to strictly condemn us.

The Bible tells us in First John chapter 5 that if we believe that Jesus Christ is God and that He died on the Cross for our sins, then we have the Holy Spirit inside of us. Jesus told us that the Holy Spirit would teach us and guide us. If we know this is true, then why are there so many Christians who say that God doesn't communicate specifically with them? The problem isn't that God isn't talking, but for some reason, people either aren't listening or don't realize that He is talking to them!

God gives us a perfect example of this type of thinking in the Bible. In First Samuel chapter 3, there is a boy named Samuel who has been dedicated to the Lord as a small child and is being raised in the temple. One night, the Lord comes to him and calls his name. Samuel hears the voice but thinks it is the priest calling him. He goes to the priest and says, "Here I am." The priest tells him that he has not called him, and he should go back and lie down. Once again the Lord calls Samuel, and once again he goes to the priest thinking that he has called him. The priest tells Samuel to go back and lie down. The third time when the Lord calls Samuel and he goes to the priest, the priest realizes it must be the Lord calling the boy. He tells him to go back and lie down and if the Lord calls again, he should say, "Speak Lord, for your servant is listening." The fourth time the Lord speaks to Samuel, he replies as the priest instructed him. The Lord then gives him a message about what was going to happen in the future.

This encouraging story shows that even someone raised in the temple (or church) could not initially discern the voice of God. So why should we be surprised or disappointed when we don't always realize when God is talking to us? Like Samuel, we might not expect to hear from God. Like Tim, we might think that His voice will be readily identifiable—unmistakable. Maybe there are too many other thoughts or distractions in our minds that are louder, competing with God for our attention. We are told in First Kings 19:11-13 that God spoke to Elijah not in a strong wind, an earthquake, or a fire, but in a gentle whisper. This is very significant because the Bible also tells us that God is constant and unchanging. This means that, when God speaks to us, we should usually expect a gentle whisper. If you or I were to say that a thought popped into our minds, what would that sound like? Wouldn't if be fair to say that it could be compared to a gentle whisper?

Jesus tells us more about the Holy Spirit in John 16:8-15. He first tells us that the Holy Spirit will convict the world regarding sin. In other words, the Holy Spirit will act as our conscience—that bad feeling we get inside when we know that we are doing something wrong. Jesus says that the Holy Spirit will reveal God's standard of righteousness to believers. He will not only tell us what is wrong, but He will also let us know what is right and what He expects. This is that good feeling we get when we are doing something that we know is right. Near the end of these verses in John chapter 16, Jesus tells us that the Holy Spirit will demonstrate Christ's judgment over satan and will guide us into all truth. We are told in other areas of the Bible that the main truth that the Holy Spirit guides us into is the truth that Jesus is God and that He died for our sins (see 1 John 5:6-12).

John 16:13 tells us that the Holy Spirit will tell us what is yet to come. This can be taken in an eternal sense. When we believe in Jesus and believe that He died for our sins, we can be assured of eternal life in Heaven. This can also be taken in an everyday sense. There have been times when the Holy Spirit told me what was going to happen to help me, my family, or others. You read earlier about the time when God showed me in a dream (or vision) how my annual review was going to turn out. He told me not to be foolish but to be patient, because I had previously decided to quit if I didn't get what I wanted. This is a good example of how the Holy Spirit can tell us or warn us about something that will happen in the future.

The Holy Spirit helped me again in this way while my wife and I were driving to church one night. We were on a twisty two-lane back road that also went up and down some small hills. As I was driving toward the top of a hill, I heard the Holy Spirit whisper that there were deer nearby and that I should be careful. I started to slow down, and I repeated out loud to my wife what I had just heard. As the car crested the hill, several deer ran out in front of the car, and we nearly hit them. If I hadn't been warned, and if I hadn't taken action to slow down, we could have been involved in a serious accident.

Another example of how the Holy Spirit tells us of what is yet to come happened when we were still living in the southern part of our state. Our entire family, including our four children, was in the car and we were traveling north for the weekend. The interstate traffic was bumper to bumper. I was driving in the passing lane next to the concrete median and going faster than I should have been.

Just as I came alongside a semitrailer truck, I heard the Holy Spirit ask me what I would do if a tire blew out. I immediately grabbed the steering wheel with both hands because I was steering with my left thumb and index finger at the time. I assumed the blowout was going to be on our van. As soon as I got both hands on the steering wheel, one of the tires on the semitrailer truck blew out and rubber smashed onto our windshield. Even though I had been warned, I still jerked the steering wheel when the rubber hit our windshield. I came within mere inches of hitting the concrete median while traveling at 70 miles per hour. If I hadn't received warning from the Holy Spirit and grabbed the steering wheel with both hands, tragedy surely would have been the result. I am so thankful that, once again, God spoke through the Holy Spirit to prepare me for what was about to happen.

GOD'S VOICE?

I had no doubt that these three experiences were the result of God speaking to me through the Holy Spirit. But sometimes His promptings are harder to discern. One day, as I was traveling to a job site in another town, I saw two crosses by the side of the road near a railroad crossing. I slowed down because I had a thought that I should stop and read the names on the crosses. One cross was freshly painted and the other was faded. I was able to read the name on the freshly painted cross, but I couldn't make out the name on the other cross. Something kept telling me to stop so I could read the name, but I was on a time schedule and didn't want to be late for my job. I slowed down almost to a stop but still couldn't read the name. At that point, another thought came to my mind, "What does it matter whose name is on the cross?" I didn't want to be late, and it didn't seem to matter, so I continued on my way to work.

On the way home that evening, I approached the railroad crossing area from the opposite direction. Once again I was prompted to stop and read the name on the faded cross, but I was running late and knew I didn't have time to stop if I was going to get to church on time for a meeting. Once again I argued with the notion because I didn't want to be late and it seemed silly. I came to a complete stop and tried to read the name from the truck. The prompting persisted until I finally got out of my truck and walked close enough to read the name on the cross. I didn't recognize the name, and it meant absolutely nothing to me. I got back into my truck thinking that I must be crazy for wasting time when I was already late.

After taking a quick shower and wolfing down supper, I arrived at the church for the evangelism committee meeting. After training exercises, we usually make encouragement visits to those with particular needs. This night there were two visits to make. Our pastor sets up the visits beforehand and then decides who is going to go on the calls based on which evangelism members are present and what the circumstances are. He hands us a card with a name and address on it, along with a phone number and a little background information.

That night at church, the pastor handed my partner the card and then told us that we were going to visit a woman who had not been in church for a while. He went on to say that there had been a death in the family some time ago and that, after the death, the woman had not attended church regularly. We were going to visit the woman to offer support and to tell her that she was missed in church. My partner handed me the card, and I noticed that the last name was the same as the one on the faded cross. The pastor told us that the woman's young daughter had died in a traffic accident. I knew in my heart that her name was the one that I had read on the cross that day, and I started to cry when the pastor verified it. I told our small group what had happened earlier that day and how I almost didn't take the time to read the name.

My partner and I visited the woman at her house. After we talked for a while, I told her what had happened earlier that day at the railroad crossing. She sat there looking at me for a while before she spoke. It was as if she was trying to decide if she should believe me or not. When she finally spoke, she asked me a question that I was not ready for. "So why do you think God wanted you to read the name on that cross today?" The Holy Spirit gave me the answer as soon as she asked the question. I told her that God wanted to show that He hadn't forgotten about her daughter or her and to let her know that He loved her and was reaching out to her in love through us. The woman burst into tears, and so did I. We had a genuine conversation, after that, based on His love and real life issues that mattered. I wish I could say that all the home visits we make are that powerful.

When I felt a prompting to read the name on the cross, it made no sense to me at all. I had no way of knowing why it would matter. My busy schedule and personal agenda seemed much more important than reading the name on a faded cross on the side of the road. Obviously, I did not realize that it was God or the Holy Spirit trying to get me to read the cross, or I wouldn't have hesitated. This shows how easy it is to drown out the voice of God during our day-to-day life. I didn't stop the first time I was prompted, and I almost didn't stop the second time—I almost missed the opportunity to help God bring healing to a grieving mother.

Thankfully, God will often repeat Himself if necessary. If you're like me, it may take more than one time before you listen closely enough to hear Him. I can think of many times when God has told me the same thing in various ways, just to make sure He was getting His point across to me. Unfortunately, I can also think of several times in my life when I didn't listen, even after I was told something more than once. Often this leads to unfortunate consequences.

The first time that I ignored the voice of God was also the first time that I heard Him speak audibly. I was 19 years old and was visiting my girlfriend for the weekend at the college she was attending in another town. We fought so much on Saturday about my doing drugs that I decided to drive home instead of staying over until Sunday evening as planned. She told me that she would drop the subject if I agreed to go to church with her on Sunday morning. I agreed but told her I'd be leaving right after the church services ended. We walked to church that morning, and as we were about to enter the building, I felt an overwhelming presence of God. It had always made me feel good in the past, but this time it made me feel very convicted about my actions. We went in and sat down in the next-to-last row. The service started, and just as we began to sing the first hymn, I heard God speak my name. That's all He said, just my name. Just in case you're wondering—yes, I was completely sober.

It was so very loud that it felt as if the whole building shook when I heard it. I can't say that it was like a yell, yet it was more powerful than anything I had ever heard before. Psalm 29:4 explains it, "The voice of the Lord is powerful; the voice of the Lord is majestic." I dropped the hymnal and spun around to look behind me when it happened. The few people who were in the back row were looking at me like I was crazy. I realized that I was the only one who heard God's voice, although it didn't seem possible because it was so loud.

Although all I heard was my name, it spoke volumes to me. Through only the sound of my name, I also heard and felt, "Bruce, I love you. Bruce, I'm concerned for you," like a parent would say to a child who was making a bad decision. I was being called and comforted and convicted all in the same breath. Someone had recently offered to help pay my way through college, and I knew that this voice was also calling me to be involved with ministry.

When the church service was over, I said good-bye to my girlfriend and quickly left. I had some pot in my car, and I started smoking it as soon as I merged onto the interstate. I kept smoking and smoking, trying to forget what had happened, but I couldn't.

I wish I could say that I listened to God that day, but I can't. I didn't quit doing or selling drugs at that point, and I definitely didn't choose to go into the ministry. Instead, I chose to listen to the other voices, the ones that told me I wasn't worthy or loved. Many times I have regretted my choice that day, or thought about the fact that I ran away from the Maker of the universe. My bad decision caused me years of heartache and pain. One would think that I should have learned a lesson about listening to God, but I continued to try to do things my own way sometimes.

Years later, the day before my brother's wife died, God told me to go to their house and spend some time with them. Two people had called me that day and asked me questions only my brother could help me answer. On that particular day, I was having a hard time fighting my addiction. I knew without a doubt that it was the Holy Spirit urging me to go talk with them, but I was fighting against Him. My brother and his wife had recently moved into their first home, and my wife and I had bought a house-warming gift for them. As a compromise with God, I decided to drop off the present on their front steps before they got home from work, so I wouldn't have to talk to them. It wasn't that I didn't want to spend time with them. I just didn't feel like talking to anybody because I was feeling so miserable. I told God that I would talk to them another day.

When I sat the present in front of their door, I clearly heard an evil voice say that she wasn't going to use the gift—not even one time.

It was so clear, that I questioned why not, to which I received no response. I am embarrassed to admit that I became angry as I thought of all the reasons why she might not use the present. That evil voice, that demon, was right; she never did get to use that present, but not because of any of the reasons that I thought of. The Bible tells us that the devil and his demons can't see into the future, but they do plan ahead and can sometimes guess how we are going to react. The book of Job gives examples of this.

Again I refer to the cartoon of an angel on one shoulder and a devil on the other. I clearly heard both of those voices that afternoon; but because I was relying on my own reasoning, I didn't follow God's will for me that day. "For our struggle is not against flesh and blood, but against the rulers, against the authorities, against the powers of this dark world and against the spiritual forces of evil in the heavenly realms" (Eph. 6:12). I can never go back and change the outcome of what happened, but I thank God that I can go to the foot of the Cross and ask for forgiveness. Even if your disobedience has tragic consequences, God will forgive you if you ask. He is faithful to forgive your sins through His grace and mercy. We don't deserve His love, yet His love is eternal. He loves us in spite of our flaws and failures. I know—He has forgiven me many times and has given me opportunities to return to His will for my life. Sometimes taking our own path and failing makes it easier to follow His will when we have seen the outcome of the alternative.

OBEDIENCE

Now, when the Holy Spirit prompts me to do something, I immediately try to obey. For instance, in the past few years, I can think of several times when I had no idea what was going on in another person's life when God had me call at just the right time with the right message for them:

- A customer's son died unexpectedly, and I called the next day.

- Many times, someone was having a really bad day, and I called right when they needed someone to talk to.

- A man's wife was in the hospital and expected to die, and I called the following day.

- I was reading a book, and God prompted me to share a certain part with a person, and it made a big difference in his life.

- The Holy Spirit prompted my wife and I to give one of our vehicles to someone who was trying to raise money for a mission trip, and then we learned that he had sold his vehicle, for money for the trip, that same day.

- God told me to pray for a couple's marriage before they even mentioned that they were struggling.

- God told me to share a certain Bible verse with someone without knowing why, and then they told me how much it meant to them.

I can take no credit for any of these things; all glory goes to God. Let me also say that, if He can use *me*, He can use anyone who is willing to listen to His promptings.

One day, I was eating lunch with a friend when my cell phone rang. It was the associate pastor from my church calling. He said that he had just heard the voice of God for the first time regarding a specific task and that he was supposed to call me, but he wasn't sure why. I thought that I knew why. I had been sober for the longest period in my adult life, about three months, but I had given in to temptation the day before. I felt horrible because of it and was having a hard time getting past it. The pastor told me that he had been singing hymns and praying and asking for forgiveness because he too had recently fallen in a weak area of his life and that God had told him to call me and tell me about it. I replied that the call must be for both of us.

We talked about some verses that deal with confession and how healthy it is to bring our sins into the light. I really respect my pastors, and for one of them to call and tell me that he had just fallen in a sin at the same time when I was dealing with guilt really made me feel better. We said our good-byes, and I was thanking God for the call when my phone rang again. It was the same pastor saying that the Lord had given him a verse from a hymn to share with me. The verse read, "Nothing that you've done remains, only what you do for me." God helped both of us feel better that day because my pastor obeyed the voice of God, even when it didn't make sense to him at first.

SIGNS

Most of the time, when I hear the Holy Spirit, He sounds like a small whisper or voice in my head. I am now at a point in my walk with the Lord when I can usually discern His voice from the other thoughts rolling around in my head. Jesus told us that His sheep will know His voice and will listen to it.

I recently drove by some friends' property that has a billboard on it. Periodically they change the motivational phrases that are displayed on it. That day, I was not paying much attention and didn't start reading the sign until I was almost past, so I could only read the first line. The Holy Spirit asked me what the sign said, and I couldn't answer because I didn't read the whole statement. He asked me the question again and then told me that the sign didn't say what it was supposed to say.

I knew it was the Holy Spirit, so I called my friend's cell phone to ask him what the sign said. I left my question on his voice mail. He called me back just minutes later. He said that he had been on the phone with someone else who had called to tell him that some prankster had changed the message on his sign to say something inappropriate. He was out of state at the time and asked if I would go back and remove the inappropriate message. I was only a few miles past the sign at that point, so I turned around and changed the sign in short order.

If I had ignored this prompting by the Holy Spirit, the sign would not have been changed as quickly as it was. The thought or voice I heard made no sense to me, but I obeyed it because God always sees the big picture. He knew why I should read the name on the faded cross, why I should have talked to my brother and his wife, why my pastor called to confess his sin, why Tim kept calling me, and the reason for all the other times when He has prompted me to call someone for no apparent (to me) reason. Only God knows everything, and He is the only one who can guide us to do His will. Sometimes the Lord might tell us to do or say something that we don't understand initially—this is where faith comes in. We can't try to rely on our own reasoning or understanding; if we do, we will fail.

HOLY SPIRIT GIFTS AND FRUIT

Jesus promised to send the Holy Spirit to His believers. You have read examples of how the Holy Spirit has spoken to me and other believers. Now I would like to take a look at some of the gifts and fruits that we can expect from the Holy Spirit. God uses these gifts and fruits in believers to minister to each other and to unbelievers. By doing this, He shows and tells about His love for all people. We are told about the fruit of the Holy Spirit in Galatians 5:22-23:

But the fruit of the Spirit is

- *love,*

- *joy,*

- *peace,*

- *patience,*

- *kindness,*

- *goodness,*

- *faithfulness,*

- *gentleness and*

- *self-control. Against such things there is no law.*

This tells us that, when we are living a life led by the Holy Spirit, He is going to start cultivating these traits in us. In nature, fruit does not appear instantly on a tree; it takes time to grow and be nurtured. It is the same way for the fruit of the Spirit. They take time to ripen in our lives. If you look at that list again, I'm sure you can think of people who have some of this fruit. The people I can think of are all mature Christians. It takes time to grow fruit in our lives.

When we apply this fruit to our daily lives, we are doing God's work here on earth. God speaks through us when we truly love our neighbors, our enemies, and our family members. When we are patient with the person at work who truly tries our patience, others will see and hear God through our actions and reactions. When we have peace and joy, even though our circumstances are anything but good, it proves to those around us that God is alive and well and that He is willing to help His followers. The Holy Spirit cultivates fruit in our lives, and He uses it to speak to those around us about the very nature of God.

The Holy Spirit also uses what the Bible calls "spiritual gifts" for the common good of all. Some spiritual gifts are listed in Romans 12:6-8:

We have different gifts, according to the grace given us. If a man's gift is

- *prophesying, let him use it in proportion to his faith. If it is*

- *serving, let him serve; if it is*

- *teaching, let him teach; if it is*

- *encouraging, let him encourage; if it is*

- *contributing to the needs of others, let him give generously; if it is*

- *leadership, let him govern diligently; if it is*

- *showing mercy, let him do it cheerfully.*

Another place in the Bible that mentions gifts of the Holy Spirit is in Ephesians 4:11-12. Here we are told:

It was He who gave some to be

- *apostles, some to be*

- *prophets, some to be*

- *evangelists, and some to be*

- *pastors and*

- *teachers, to prepare God's people for works of service, so that the body of Christ may be built up.*

The last verse of this passage is very important. It tells us again the purpose of these spiritual gifts. We read that these spiritual fruits and gifts are to prepare God's people for works of service, so that the

Body of Christ, the Church Body, may be built up. Fruit and gifts are not for the benefit of the one who has them, but they are for the people around them. Fruit and gifts are given to prepare the one entrusted with them for works of service. They are not given to boost spiritual pride. On the contrary, they are given so that person is better equipped to serve others.

Spiritual gifts are also mentioned in First Corinthians 12:4-11. It starts by giving the reason for these gifts:

> *There are different kinds of gifts, but the same Spirit. There are different kinds of service, but the same Lord. There are different kinds of working, but the same God works all of them in all men. Now to each one the manifestation of the Spirit is given for the common good. To one there is given through the Spirit the*

- *message of wisdom, to another the*

- *message of knowledge by means of the same Spirit, to another*

- *faith by the same Spirit, to another*

- *gifts of healing by that one Spirit, to another*

- *miraculous powers, to another*

- *prophecy, to another*

- *distinguishing between spirits, to another*

- *speaking in different kinds of tongues, and to still another the*

- *interpretation of tongues. All these are the work of one and the same Spirit, and He gives them to each one, just as He determines.*

This last list of gifts is intriguing, but the remainder of the chapter makes it very clear that no gift is sufficient to stand by itself. The writer compares the Church, or the Body of Christ, to a physical body. Just as your physical body is made up of many different parts, so is the Body of Christ. Each part of your physical body plays an important role in your overall health—so does each part of the Church Body. There is no room for pride or envy. There are no "super Christians," just as there are no "surplus Christians." The person who has been given the gift of healing is no more important than the person who has been given the gift of strong faith. Paul tells us in the next chapter of First Corinthians that no gift is effective or worthwhile without love. He follows this by saying that we should eagerly desire the spiritual gifts.

The book of Acts speaks directly about the Holy Spirit and shows how there were a few different ways that people received this filling of the Spirit (sometimes called a baptism or anointing of the Holy Spirit). On the Day of Pentecost, 3,000 people came to faith and received the Holy Spirit by hearing the Word and being baptized. Cornelius, a Gentile, and his group also received the Holy Spirit just by hearing the Word (before they were water baptized). (See Acts 2:1-41; 10:44-48.) We read in other places of people who had been baptized but still did not receive this filling of the Holy Spirit until God's messenger laid their hands on them and prayed over them, specifically asking for the Holy Spirit to fill them. (See Acts 8:14-17; 9:17-19; 19:1-7.) The most important thing to keep in mind, and the one thing that is common to all of these fillings of the Holy Spirit, is that the person being filled truly desires to be filled by the Holy Spirit. He or she repents, confesses, turns away from their sin, and claims the forgiveness offered by the death of Jesus as their own.

We can take Jesus's words at full face value in Luke 11:13, "If you then, though you are evil, know how to give good gifts to your children, how much more will your Father in heaven give the Holy Spirit to those who ask Him!" God wants to give you the gift of His

Spirit. Because God made us unique, and talks to us individually, we can understand why there are different reactions to being anointed by the Holy Spirit. Many people say that they physically felt a filling or indwelling of the Holy Spirit when it happened while others do not. Some people have an immediate reaction while others have a delayed reaction. It often takes prayer and discernment to realize what gifts you have been given, but we need to remember Jesus's words in the previous verse. (See Luke 11:13.) God will answer your prayer for the Holy Spirit because it is in line with His will and glorifies Him. We don't need to be concerned with how much of the Holy Spirit we have, but how much He has of us. Walking with God is a life-long journey, not a Sunday morning vacation. The more we humble ourselves and become daily obedient to Him, the more of His fruit and gifts He will bless us with. As this process continues, we will more clearly hear or discern His voice, and those around us will also hear God speak to them through our lives.

YOUR TURN

Write about the fruit or gifts you have been given. If you haven't prayed for the filling of the Holy Spirit yet, I urge you to do so. God loves to answer this prayer! Write about some times in your life when God spoke to you through the Holy Spirit. Maybe it was an audible voice, or maybe it was a thought or prompting that came into your mind that you know was not your own.

_____

_____

_____

_____

_____

_____

_____

_____

_____

_____

_____

_____

_____

STUDY QUESTIONS

1. Jesus gave the Great Commission in Matthew 28:18-20, show-ing us the triune nature of God and promising to be with us al-ways. How will Jesus be with us always? (See John 14:15-19, 25-26; 16:7,13.)

2. List the seven things that Jesus promised the Holy Spirit will do for us, in us, and through us. (See John 14:17, 14:26 this verse has (2) items, 16:8, 16:13 this verse has (2) items, 16:14.)

3. Ten days after Jesus ascended into Heaven, on Pentecost, God made the Holy Spirit available to all believers (see Acts 2). Who (what types of people or positions) was the Holy Spirit available to in the Old Testament? (See Exodus 40:12-15; Judges 3:9-10; 13:2-5,24-25; First Samuel 3:19-21; 16:1-13.)

4. Who is He available to today and why? (See Acts 2:17-18; Hebrews 13:8; Malachi 3:6; Ephesians 1:13-14; First John 5; Luke 11:13.)

5. What does the Holy Spirit sound like? (See First Kings 19:11-13.)

6. Reread the story of Tim. What did Tim learn?

7. What does a whisper sound like? What does the cartoon analogy teach us about the thoughts that come into our minds?

8. Jesus clearly promised to speak to us (see John 8:47; 10:27). Why, then, do so many Christians honestly believe God does not speak specifically to them?

9. What can you learn about discernment from the story of the crosses?

10. First Samuel 3:1-11 gives an example of someone who, though raised in the Church, did not automatically discern the voice of God. Why is this often true?

    ▪ a.

    ▪ b.

    ▪ c.

11. What does the story about my hearing God in church tell us about human nature? What Bible stories also demonstrate this truth?

JOURNAL

CHAPTER 6

GOD TALKS THROUGH DESIGN AND CIRCUMSTANCE

WE ARE TOLD IN THE VERY FIRST VERSE OF THE BIBLE THAT "In the beginning God created the heavens and the earth" (Gen. 1:1). The remainder of this first chapter of the Bible tells us in what order He created all things. Day one, He created light, so that there was day and night. Day two, He separated the waters in the heavens from the waters on the earth and created the sky. Day three, He gathered together the waters on the earth and formed the seas, and the dry ground He called land. He also created all vegetation that day. Day four, He created the sun, moon, and stars to govern the day and the night and to mark the seasons. Day five, He created the fish and the birds to fill the waters and the sky. On the sixth day, God created animals to fill the earth and man and woman to care for the earth and commune with God. On the seventh day, God rested and declared all He had made to be very good.

What a magnificent world God has created! God speaks loudly to us simply through His creation. Look at the world around you—it is quite amazing. Psalm 19:1-4 says,

The heavens declare the glory of God; the skies proclaim the work of His hands. Day after day they pour forth speech; night after night they display knowledge. There is no speech or language where their voice is not heard. Their voice goes out into all the earth, their words to the ends of the world....

God reveals Himself to us through nature. We see a God of order and beauty and detail—a God who is intelligent and powerful. This kind of speaking to us is known as *general revelation*. Paul explained it this way:

Since what may be known about God is plain to them, because God has made it plain to them. For since the creation of the world God's invisible qualities—His eternal power and divine nature—have been clearly seen, being understood from what has been made, so that men are without excuse (Romans 1:19-20).

In other words, when we look at creation, it's obvious that there is a Creator. We see that even ancient civilizations worldwide acknowledged that some higher power, or God, was behind the scenes of life. The Bible reveals exactly who the God of creation is and what He is all about. This is known as *special revelation*.

Creation was perfect until Adam and Eve sinned. After "the fall," even nature became cursed. Thorns and thistles appeared, and man had to work the land in order to survive. Natural disasters came into being, and nature was out of balance. (See Genesis 2–3.) Both man and nature will have to wait until the end of this world to become perfect again.

The creation waits in eager expectation for the sons of God to be revealed. For the creation was subjected to frustration, not by its own choice, but by the will of the

One who subjected it, in hope that the creation itself will be liberated from its bondage to decay and brought into the glorious freedom of the children of God. We know that the whole creation has been groaning as in the pains of childbirth right up to the present time. Not only so, but we ourselves, who have the firstfruits of the Spirit, groan inwardly as we wait eagerly for our adoption as sons, the redemption of our bodies (Romans 8:19-23).

In Revelation, the last book of the Bible, we are told that God will make a new Heaven and a new earth—the previous passage from Romans says that creation has been eagerly waiting for this. Creation will again be perfect and so will all the people who live there. We are told that it will be even better than we can imagine. God will live with His people, and all will be right:

And I heard a loud voice from the throne saying, "Now the dwelling of God is with men, and He will live with them. They will be His people, and God Himself will be with them and be their God. He will wipe away every tear from their eyes. There will be no more death or mourning or crying or pain, for the old order of things has passed away" (Revelation 21:3-4).

This sounds like a great place to be!

Even though creation is still under a curse, for now, we can hear God speaking to us through it. Most people who have had pets will vouch for the unconditional love that God puts inside of them. When we see people or animals protecting their young, even unto death, we see a picture of God's love for us. The glory of a sunrise, the majesty of the mountains, the splendor of the seas, all proclaim a message from God. God uses creation to talk to us!

Our Lord God says that He is the Alpha and the Omega, the beginning and the end. (See Revelation 22:13.) It's no coincidence that He calls Himself this and that He began and will end the world as we know it. It's also no coincidence that He begins and ends the Bible the way that He does. All the bad things that we find at the beginning of the Bible are cured for eternity at the end of the Bible. At the beginning of the Bible, sin enters creation through satan, people are cursed and hide from God, tears are shed, and paradise is lost. At the end of the Bible, satan is defeated, sin is banished, people are blessed and live with God for eternity, there are no more tears, and paradise is regained.

JESUS AND JOSEPH

God talks to us through His creation or design, and His design affects our circumstances. For example, we don't choose what country we will be born in, what government is in power, what color we will be, or what our family will be like. (Look up Acts 17:26 and Psalm 33:11 to see who does.) Some people call these things fate, or uncontrollable circumstances. The Bible says that God designed and planned *all* things. "In Him we were also chosen, having been pre-destined according to the plan of Him who works out everything in conformity with the purpose of His will" (Eph. 1:11).

God gives all human beings free will, and therefore, we can make our own choices about a lot of things in life. God also knows what choices each one of us will make. Because He knows what we will do, He works out everything that He wants accomplished in the long run, despite our bad choices or decisions. We are given many examples of this in the Bible. The best example is Jesus. He lived a perfect life without sin, yet He was tortured and crucified. His circumstances do not seem fair or justified to our way of thinking. But Jesus shed His innocent blood for our sins. He was sacrificed so we could live forever in Heaven. This is a perfect example of God talking to one of His children and accomplishing His will, despite unjust circumstances.

Maybe you're thinking that it was different for Jesus because He was God. Maybe you think that, because you're an everyday person, God's not worried about or in control of your circumstances. Not true. He cares about everyday people—like Joseph. Joseph wasn't perfect; he had family problems, and a lot of unfair things happened to him. But God used Joseph's circumstances to accomplish His will, even though they weren't right or just in our way of thinking.

The story of Joseph is told in the book of Genesis chapters 37 through 50. He was favored by his father and had received a richly ornamented robe from him. In his dreams, his family was bowing to him, and Joseph bragged about these dreams. Because of these things, his brothers were jealous and hated him. His father sent Joseph to check on his brothers one day, and when they saw him coming, they devised a plan to get rid of him. They threw him into a cistern and then debated about what to do with him. At that time, some merchants came by, so they sold Joseph to them. He was taken to Egypt and sold as a slave to one of the pharaoh's officials, Potiphar.

God blessed Joseph's hard work, and his master put him in charge of everything in the household. But Potiphar's wife wanted Joseph to sleep with her, though he refused. One day, she tried to seduce him, and he ran away from her. She became angry and accused him of trying to rape her. He was thrown into prison for a crime he did not commit.

While he was in prison, he interpreted two dreams for two of the pharaoh's officials. Both interpretations came true. Two years later, the pharaoh had two dreams that no one could interpret. One official remembered how Joseph had accurately interpreted previous dreams. The pharaoh sent for Joseph, who was still in prison, and he interpreted both of the pharaoh's dreams, with God's help.

Although the dreams were different, they both meant the same thing. The dreams foretold seven years of abundance, followed by seven years of famine. Joseph told the pharaoh how he should prepare for the upcoming events, and the pharaoh put Joseph in charge of the entire country. Joseph devised a way to store the food during the abundant years, and when the famine came, he distributed the food throughout Egypt. Because the famine affected that entire part of the world, Joseph's family was also out of food. His father sent his brothers to buy food from Egypt, because it was the only country that had food.

Joseph recognized his brothers, but they did not recognize him. Joseph told them that he thought they were spies and kept one of them in jail until they brought back their youngest brother to prove their story. He sent food home with the nine brothers. When they returned months later, he told them who he was and asked them to bring his father to him so they could all live together in Egypt. He would supply their needs and they would be saved from the famine.

Only our living God could write an ending like that! God used seemingly hopeless circumstances to accomplish His will. He turned Joseph's life around, and He will do the same for you. The Bible doesn't mention that Joseph ever had a bad attitude or that he became angry with God. On the contrary, it says that he worked hard and was diligent, no matter what he was doing.

We know that Joseph's heart was in the right place when he told his brothers, "Don't be afraid. Am I in the place of God? You intended to harm me, but God intended it for good to accomplish what is now being done, the saving of many lives" (Gen. 50:19-20).

HIS DESIGN, OUR CIRCUMSTANCES

It took a while for God's plan for Joseph to play out, but in the end, Joseph realized that his life full of bad circumstances was working toward eternal joy. Are you in the middle of some bad circumstances? Have you ever faced troubling circumstances and later realized that God worked it out for your benefit? Maybe you lost your job, but then you were offered a better one. Maybe you had a health problem that caused you to change your lifestyle, and now you are happier and healthier. Maybe you lost a loved one, and now you value much more the time that you share with family and friends. The list of ways that God can turn bad to good is endless—we must have faith.

Paul wrote, "And we know that in *all* things God works for the good of those who love Him, who have been called according to His purpose" (Rom. 8:28). Please notice that the verse says *all* things, not some things. This can be a very hard teaching to take to heart, especially when we are in the middle of those bad circumstances and can't (or won't) see any possible good coming from them. Unfortunately, sometimes it takes years to see the good that God has planned. What can be even more disheartening is when we don't see the good result during our lifetime. Our lifetime is barely a blink compared to eternity—God's plan and purpose are woven throughout generations.

Sometimes God lets bad circumstances come our way so we can comfort and console someone who is facing the same circumstances at a later time. If we haven't been through the trial ourselves, we can't truly relate to others in trouble. Having overcome rough times, we can witness that God helped us through and that He will never let us down. We can share our Christian perspective with people, and they may come to a saving relationship with God just because they understand that we understand their circumstances. We can't always control other people, our circumstances, or even ourselves. In the end, we have to trust God like Jesus and Joseph did, or we will fail by trusting in our own devices.

God is our loving Father, and sometimes He would rather strengthen us in the middle of our pain rather than deliver us from it. Often our bad circumstances are the very things God can most easily use to help us grow closer to Him. God strengthens us through His Holy Spirit, the Bible, and other Christians. Only God knows what our limits are and what we can handle. We are told in Second Corinthians 4:8-9, "We are hard pressed on every side, but not crushed; perplexed, but not in despair; persecuted, but not abandoned; struck down, but not destroyed." God doesn't promise that our life with Him will be a bowl full of cherries, but He does promise that He will help us get through it!

"The Lord is close to the brokenhearted and saves those who are crushed in spirit. A righteous man may have many troubles, but the Lord delivers him from them all" (Ps. 34:18-19). These words can be of comfort when we can't see God's hand in a situation.

These days, there are many natural disasters happening worldwide. There are economic upheavals when people lose their jobs. Families are reeling from the affects of divorce, substance abuse, sexual abuse, and abortion. There is government waste and rising costs for food, gas, heating oil, and much more. Wars and serious conflicts plague many parts of the world. Disease and sickness are killing thousands. Even when things are looking bleak, we have to trust God and believe His promises.

A good example of trusting God through tragic circumstances is the story of Job. Job had it all—property, family, possessions, and good health—and then he lost it all. His children, his possessions, and finally his health were all taken from him. His wife told him to curse God for all that had happened, but he responded with these wise words, "You are talking like a foolish woman. Shall we accept good from God, and not trouble?" (Job 2:10). Job saw that God was in control of everything, even when he didn't understand his circumstances.

We often evaluate ourselves and our relationship with God based on our surroundings and circumstances. It's easy to take pride in what we have, or in our accomplishments, rather than in what God has done for us. It's also easy to blame God when things fall apart. Job's friends told him that he must have sinned greatly to have so many bad things happen to him. But they find out later that sin was not the reason; Job was being tested. Job's friends actually sinned by judging his circumstances!

Our circumstances are usually our own doing. Because of our sins, mistakes, and bad decisions, we often have to deal with the consequences. For instance, if a person decides to have sex outside of marriage or to have an adulterous affair, that person is susceptible to contracting a sexually transmitted disease. Using illegal drugs may lead to addiction, arrest, or death. Drinking alcohol and driving may cause an accident or the loss of driving privileges. Most of the time, we make the choices that cause either good or bad consequences.

But sometimes, like Joseph, we have to suffer the consequences of somebody else's sin. This can be tough to swallow; but if we have a relationship with God, we can fall back on Him during dark times. I was angry at God for many years for allowing me to be molested as a child. Because He had answered my prayer and hugged me the night when I prayed, I knew He was powerful and real. But this almost made it worse for me because I couldn't understand how a God who was so real would allow bad things to happen.

BUILDING TESTIMONY

It took more than 20 years before I could see that God could use bad circumstances in my life for the benefit of His Kingdom. We need to remember that God is not the author of the bad things that happen in our life, but He is big enough to use them for good when given the opportunity. When I share the story about when Jesus hugged me, I see how it affects people and increases their belief in God. The same thing happens when I recount how the angels came to my rescue. When we tell others how real God is to us, and how he helps us daily, people listen—they are encouraged. Life can be tough, and we all need hope. It's rewarding when we get to see right away how God uses circumstances to help us. If we give God the credit, it builds our faith and helps our testimony to others.

I lived in a large city while going to college. For the first year, I stayed in a large, low-income apartment complex in the heart of the city. There was a lot of crime, and almost every night police helicopters flew overhead and lit up the area with bright lights. Very often, in the morning, I saw one or two vehicles that had been stripped down or vandalized. With no warning, gunshots and sirens pierced the air. One night I came home from work at about midnight. Someone had taken "my" parking spot, and I had to park on the other side of the row that night. I always backed my truck into the parking spot so I could just pull out when I left. My apartment was on the ground level, and I had a corner unit at one end of the building.

When I backed my truck into the only available stall which was on the other side of the lot, my headlights shone on a man who was hiding in the bushes next to my apartment door. I watched him for a moment and then shut off my truck engine. He never moved. I carried a large hunting knife in my truck, and I decided that I should get it out in case I had to protect myself. I walked slowly toward my door, and when I got close, the man came out from behind the bushes toward me. I showed him the knife in my hand and told him not to do anything foolish. I think he was on drugs because he was acting oddly and wasn't scared of the knife. Fortunately, though, it kept him at bay until I could get safely inside my apartment.

When I pulled into the parking lot that night, I was angry that someone had taken my usual parking spot, but if my normal spot had been available, I would not have seen the man lurking in the shadows. I believe God used that irritating circumstance to protect me from harm.

Remember when I told you about keeping a list of *answered* prayers? I told you that I also had kept a list of *unanswered* prayers, and on that list was a selfish prayer. I started bowhunting whitetail deer when I was 12 years old. I have continued to bowhunt almost every year, except during the period of time when I lived in another state and when I first got married. I harvested many deer and a few bucks, but never a trophy buck. I prayed to harvest a trophy buck more times than I can count for three decades, but I rarely even saw a trophy buck. After all the miraculous things that God had done, and all the countless prayers that He had already answered for me, I knew without a shadow of a doubt that He could send a trophy buck my way. But He didn't—until October 22, 2003, when He sent two.

This particular day I was perched in a tree stand on the land right by our house. I heard a deer walking through the woods behind me, and all of a sudden I saw a beautiful 8-point buck. I watched him eat acorns for a while, and I was thanking God for this long-awaited opportunity. Then a huge 10-point buck walked up and pressured the 8-pointer away from the acorns. The 10-pointer was now directly below me, and the 8-pointer was 15 yards away and standing broadside to me. It was a perfect shot for the 8-pointer, but I decided I would try a shot at the 10-pointer instead. That little voice in my head said, "Don't be greedy," but I didn't listen. I took a bad shot at the 10-pointer and ended up with neither.

I was crushed. For me to want something so badly for so long and not be able to attain it, no matter how hard I tried, was very frustrating. I reasoned that God was not answering my prayers about this because I was still occasionally using illegal drugs. I made a vow to myself that I would throw away any paraphernalia and I would stop doing drugs once and for all—which was not the first or last time that I did this. Nine days later, Halloween 2003, I was hunting from the same tree stand. The same large 8-point buck came by me, and again I was offered a good shot at it. Because I had thrown away my pot pipe and had not smoked any pot, I felt like I was doing my part. When I pulled my bow back, it broke. As much as I hate to admit it, I snapped too. I started screaming and yelling, and I threw my equipment down. I was completely beside myself with rage. I climbed down from the tree stand and went back to the house. I needed to relieve some tension, so I grabbed an ax from the garage and started chopping wildly at a stump that was in our yard.

I was angry at God. I couldn't believe that, after 20 years, He would not answer this one silly prayer. As I was chopping on the stump, I was yelling up to Him. It's the only time in my life when I remember yelling at God, and it was over something so trivial. That stump became a shameful reminder of how foolish I was that day. One year later, to the exact day, I was awakened in the middle of the night by a phone call. My dad told me that my brother's wife had died. After I hung up, I got on my knees and was praying to God for help in this situation. I was facing our bedroom window, with my folded hands on the windowsill. When I finished praying, I noticed the stump in the moonlight. God reminded me of how immature I had been, a year ago, over something so small—and He reminded me of how much I had grown in my faith since that temper tantrum. Only God knows what is in our hearts. He knows what things are truly important to us and what it will take to get through to us. He uses the design of our personalities and the desires of our hearts to talk to us through our circumstances.

Nearly ten years later, after trying for thirty years to harvest a trophy buck, I finally got one. But, it wasn't until the Lord had dealt with me and shown me that this was a type of idol to me. Once I repented and let it go it was no longer that important and I began to enjoy hunting for the gift it was, spending time in God's creation with family and friends. At that point God could trust me with getting a trophy buck and not letting it be an idol-and that is when I got it.

Think about some "small thing" that is important to you—something you really enjoy. It could be a hobby, an activity, or even watching television. Maybe it's something you do at a certain time of day, a ritual—something that's not an issue of life and death but that's still important to you. How has God used that thing to talk to you? Has He told you, like He's told me, that the something might be *too* important, that you're spending too much time on it? God does give us things for our enjoyment, but He never wants to have to compete with them for our attention. The Bible says He is a jealous God and if some activity or thing has our focus and attention more than Him, it has become an idol. I urge you to be open to God's voice and to listen to what He has to say, even about the "small things" in your life.

FOR THE SAKE OF OTHERS

Sometimes God will use someone else's circumstances to affect our lives. I told you earlier that one of my younger brothers had cancer as a small child. When he was healed, it proved to me again that God answers prayer. Although I was not the one who had cancer, God used that circumstance to help me grow in my relationship with Him. When I was much older, God used another circumstance, in someone else's life, to speak to me.

One day, as I was about to leave for a job, the customer called to cancel the appointment. I was a little disgruntled because that was the only job I had planned for the day. Since my plans had changed, I decided to call one of my suppliers for prices so that I could figure out a few estimates for other customers. I had dealt with this particular person for quite a while, and after talking for a bit, I could tell that something was wrong. When I asked if he was OK, he told me that his wife was in the hospital and that the doctors didn't know what was wrong with her—that she might die. I told him that I would include her on our prayer chain at church. After I got off the phone,

I prayed for the woman immediately. My wife called in the prayer request to our church, and we also prayed for her at a Bible study.

I called back two days later to ask the man how his wife was doing. I talked to one of his employees, and he told me that the wife had an amazing recovery—and the doctors couldn't explain it. The man wasn't at work because he was bringing his wife home from the hospital. I started praising God on the phone and explained that her sudden recovery was from answered prayer. I told him how we had been praying for her. He was silent for a while before he agreed, "It must have been answered prayer." God used this woman's illness and recovery to affect several people I know—and probably many I don't know about. It increased the faith of everyone who prayed for her when she was healed. The employee I talked to was also affected. Instead of not having an answer for her recovery, he too gave God the credit. I don't know if the woman or her husband believed that God healed her; but I can tell you that I believe it, and I believe that God used this circumstance for His glory.

There is no such thing as coincidence! Ephesians 1:11 says, "In Him we were also chosen, having been predestined according to the plan of Him who works out everything in conformity with the purpose of His will." Most of the stories I have shared with you involve a "big coincidence." Believers know that God is in control in all circumstances—having confidence in Him dispels the doubters' questions. It is no coincidence that:

1. When Bob went to church, the pastor's sermon was about the Samaritan woman.

2. The Sunday school teacher's lesson was about Jesus holding the little children.

3. I found the softball right after I prayed about it.

4. My brother's cancer was healed after praying about it.

5.   I met my wife-to-be the day after I prayed to God to send me a mate.

6.   The verses God gave me to tell Joe were also the ones in the devotional for that day.

7.   I got promoted to the manager job the day after I prayed for more money.

8.   I had a dream that showed me exactly how my annual review was going to turn out.

9.   My replacement at work showed up a few days after I prayed.

10.   The used-car manager found the truck I needed, not the one I asked for.

11.   The devotion I skipped was about the man who came home from work angry.

12.   The first verses my customer read when he opened the Bible were about trusting God.

13.   God told me about the Holy Spirit right before I heard the same sermon on the radio.

14.   The man I talked to at the gas station addressed every issue I was dealing with.

15.   I stopped and read the name on the cross the same day I went to the mother's home.

16.   My friend Tim kept calling me right before I was about to smoke pot.

17.   I thought about a tire blowout seconds before it happened.

18. I thought about deer right before they jumped out in front of our van.

19. My parking spot was taken, and I then saw the hiding man.

20. The woman was miraculously healed after we prayed for her.

BY HIS DESIGN

I am as skeptical as anyone, but I have experienced His presence firsthand. When I look at just these previous 20 stories together, it dispels any doubt I may have. God talks to everyday people, every day—not through coincidences, but through His design.

Another great example of how God talks through design happened while I was in high school and was deer hunting out of town. I was staying at a friend's house for the gun-hunting season, which was a little over a week. We were getting up very early each day and staying up late each night partying. One evening, after hunting for the day, I drove back home to see my girlfriend for a few hours. When I left, it was already after midnight, and I had about an hour drive back to the hunting grounds. I was having a hard time keeping my eyes open because I was so tired, and I finally fell asleep while driving.

The road I was on is perfectly straight for several miles. I'm not sure how long I had been sleeping when, all of a sudden, I was jerked awake by a loud noise. The exhaust pipe had broken off of the header on one side of my engine—it was an old hot rod, and the open header was extremely loud. In front of the car was a herd of deer, completely covering the road and the ditch. Because the deer were so close, I immediately swerved off the road into an open field to miss them. I ended up driving between a few deer, but I didn't hit one! If my exhaust hadn't "coincidently" broken at that exact moment, I would have driven right into that herd of deer—killing them and possibly me. If this story sounds far-fetched to you, I understand, because it sounds that way to me, and I lived it. All I can tell you is that the God we serve is incredible!

Another time that God designed a circumstance was when I was the lead mechanic at a truck garage. There was a run-ability problem on a truck that I just couldn't figure out. I was out of ideas, and my boss was starting to get uptight. I prayed to God for help as I was working on the engine. Minutes later, I dropped a small part inside the engine that I couldn't get out without disassembling the engine. I told my boss what had happened and that I didn't expect to get paid for fixing my mistake. When I took the engine apart to get out the piece that I had dropped, I discovered what the run-ability problem was. God answered my prayer with a mistake that helped solve the problem.

That's not the only time that God has used mistakes to help solve a problem. I can also think of a few mistakes that *other* people have made that revealed some of *my* problems! When I was about 8 years old, I went somewhere with my dad, and we saw some antique motorcycles. They were old tank-shift Harley Davidsons, and I was instantly infatuated. From that day on, I wanted to own one, and when I graduated from high school, I bought a 1937 model. I later bought a 1946 Harley and a 1948 Harley, both of which I restored and ended up selling, though I always kept the 1937. These antique motorcycles went from being a passion of mine to becoming an obsession. I spent all of my extra time and money on them. I would even travel to other states to try to find parts. I bought or traded for parts that I needed, even if I knew that they were stolen. I even stole a few pieces myself and justified it by telling myself that it was OK because the guy had overcharged me for some other parts.

I spent several years trying to collect the pieces that I needed to make my 1937 Harley 100 percent original. There were roughly only

1,500 of these motorcycles originally produced, and it was very hard to find the parts I needed. I had the motorcycle apart for many years before I got even close to reassembling it. When I finally had most of the parts I needed, I sent them out to be processed, re-chromed, etc. Two very important parts were wrecked at the chrome shop. "Coincidently," I had stolen one of these parts, and I had traded some stolen parts for the other part. I sent all of the hardware and small pieces that I needed to get re-plated to a different plating shop that did that type of work. When the parts were shipped back, the box was damaged, and several small pieces were missing. "Coincidently" these missing parts had questionable origins as well.

When I finally went to put the motorcycle together, I ended up "coincidently" breaking the last known stolen part for my bike. God had purged my bike of every single ill-gotten part by the time it was done. It took me a couple additional years to replace those parts, but when I did, they were 100 percent legitimate. God used these "coincidences" to teach me three very valuable lessons:

1.   God knows everything!

2.   Ill-gotten treasure is cursed!

3.   Just because time has passed doesn't mean I get away with something!

As I write this book, I think about how foolishly I've lived my life. My hope is that, by exposing my foolishness and sharing how God has corrected and guided me, you will be inspired to see God's hand in your life as well.

DESIGNED TO SERVE HIM

The next example of God's perfect design actually happened to my wife. We were married but didn't have any children yet, and she was working in a job that she didn't like. One Sunday at church, our pastor mentioned that the church daycare and preschool were going to be looking for another employee. The following day, while my wife was at work, the daycare director—by design—was in town and parked in front of my wife's workplace. My wife saw her through the window, went out to talk to her, and ended up getting the job. After we moved back to our hometown area, our church's preschool needed a part-time teacher, and my wife accepted the position—and worked there for several years. She then became co-chair of the group that oversees the preschool. It is also worth mentioning that her preschool career has been great training for mothering our four children. As you can see, God talks through design and circumstance and makes things work out for a reason.

When Lori and I got married and moved to the southern part of the state, we didn't know anyone. One of my friends from home told me that another couple from our area had moved there a few years before and that he would introduce us. Although this couple lived about an hour away, we started visiting with them regularly, taking turns driving to each other's homes. One particular Friday night, we wanted to get together, but no one wanted to make the drive. Someone suggested that we meet in the small town located roughly halfway between us. There was a bar there that served food and had some pool tables.

After we had finished eating, we played pool and had a few drinks. It was my turn to buy the drinks, and as I walked toward the bar, I saw Joe, the guy I worked with. This was during the time when he was separated from his wife and was living in the barn. He had told me previously that he had quit drinking years before and that he hadn't had a drink in a very long time. I watched as he sat down and ordered a drink. When I came up beside him, I saw that he had been crying. I told the bartender that he didn't really want that drink and that he would take a soda instead. When he heard me talk, he turned to me with a shocked look on his face and broke down sobbing. He asked me why I was there because he knew I didn't live in that area.

Before I could answer, he said, "God put you here to help me so that I wouldn't start drinking again." He said that he was having a horrible night and that he had decided that he might just as well start drinking again because he felt like nothing mattered. Because God had already designed the "coincidence" with the verses, Joe could look at this situation and see the hand of God working to help him. Praise God for His mercy and love! I hope that you are at the point where you can see that some "coincidences" are really the hand of God reaching into our daily lives. God talks to us in our day-to-day life, but we have to be willing to give Him the credit and believe that it is really His design and not just a "coincidence."

Another time, a man that I do work for had been in a long-term relationship which, despite his wishes, had ended. He was alone for a while, and then he ran into a woman that he had known for a long time. She had also been in a long-term relationship that had just ended. They started dating, and he had very strong feelings for her right away. But she broke the relationship off in a short time and went back to her previous boyfriend. My friend was hurting again, and he decided to spend time in prayer at his church. He prayed that this woman would see her boyfriend for the person that he really was. The very next day, her phone rang. The call was from her boyfriend's phone number, but when she said hello, there was no answer. Oddly, she could hear talking in the background, and she realized that it was her boyfriend talking to another woman. The things that she heard made her decide that he was not the person she should be with. God answered my friend's prayer through His design and the woman's circumstance. I have chuckled to myself more than once when I think about what happened that day. I wonder if the man bumped the speed dial button or if an angel did it? I guess it doesn't matter either way; her phone rang, and she heard what she needed to hear. My friend married her, and they are living happily together right now.

WRITE THE BOOK

The last "coincidence" that I want to share with you happened to me right before I started to write this book. Several people had told me to share these stories with others, and the last few told me that the stories should be in book form. I was really struggling with this whole idea for a few reasons. First, I was trained as a mechanic, not an author. Second, because of all the mistakes I've made and the way I've lived my life, I didn't feel worthy to tell anybody about God. I felt as if God wanted me to write it, but I also thought He was picking the wrong person.

One morning, during my daily ritual of reading a devotional, reading the Bible, and praying, the printed Scripture verses from the devotional jumped off the page and burned into my heart. This was only a few days after the last person had told me that they felt I was to write a book. I knew that God was speaking to me through these verses. "...I have chosen you and have not rejected you. So do not fear, for I am with you; do not be dismayed, for I am your God. I will strengthen you and help you; I will uphold you with My righteous right hand" (Isa. 41:9-10). I finished reading the devotional, read the suggested Bible readings, and ended with prayer.

My heart was troubled, and I decided to read the Bible for a little more comfort. Sometimes I just flip open the Bible and start reading. When I did it that day, the Bible opened to Isaiah chapter 41. My Bible has over 2,500 pages, and I "coincidently" opened it to the exact page where the devotional Scripture verses came from. I read what was on both of the open pages, and I stopped to pray again. I told God that I didn't feel worthy and that I couldn't understand why He would possibly want me to be His messenger. I closed the Bible and started to put it back on the shelf where I kept it. As I lifted it toward the shelf, a folded piece of paper fell out. It was the list of passages that I had written when I was 14 years old and my brother had cancer. I have always kept that piece of paper folded up in my Bible.

The paper landed on my desk, right in front of me. When I looked down at it, I saw that there was a star next to one of the verses. Behind the star were the verses that were printed in the devotional that day, the very same verses that I had opened my Bible up to! I am a hard-headed individual, but even I could see that God really wanted me to listen to what He was telling me. I read the verses a third time. "I have chosen you and have not rejected you. So do not fear, for I am with you; do not be dismayed, for I am your God. I will strengthen you and help you; I will uphold you with My righteous right hand." I started to write this book that very same day.

God talks to us. He talks to us through nature and His creation. He talks to us through His design, our circumstances, and what some call fate. He also talks to us through what some people mistakenly call "coincidence."

YOUR TURN

Write about the things in God's creation that God has used to talk to you. Write about circumstances in your life that God has used to talk to you or others—things that were completely out of your control. You may have called it fate, but you can now see that God used them for His purposes. Write about the times in your life when you got just what you needed, even though you didn't ask. You might have said that it was luck or a "coincidence." It might have been something good, or it could have been disciplinary, but either way, you needed it.

_____

_____

_____

_____

_____

_____

_____

_____

_____

_____

_____

_____

STUDY QUESTIONS

1. The Bible says that because God talks to us though His creation (see Gen. 1; Ps. 19:1-4), we have no excuse for not believing in God (see Rom. 1:19-20). In what ways has God spoken to you through His creation?

2. The Bible says that right now the earth is under a curse (see Gen. 3:1-21; Rom. 8:19-23). When will this curse be removed? (See Revelation 21:3-4.)

3. God's design directly affects our circumstances. Some refer to this reality as fate, uncontrollable circumstances, or coincidence. What do Ephesians 1:11 , Acts 17:26, and Psalm 33:11 say about this?

4. God did not make us robots, but gives us free will (see Deut. 28). However, because He knows what decisions we will make, He is able to accomplish His will despite human free will. How does the story of Joseph illustrate this?

5. God has called and empowered us to live in triumph and victory. Why is it that this often does not come without a struggle? (See Acts 4:22; Philippians 1:29; Hebrews 12:4-11; Romans 5:2-5; James 1:2-4; First Peter 1:6; and John 16:33.)

6. The Bible teaches that suffering and trials will happen, but that they may all be overcome. This is the "Good News" and the "Final Say." (See John 16:33; Romans 8:28; Ephesians 3:20; Second Corinthians 1:20; Mark 11:22-24; Colossian 1:13; Romans 8:37; Luke 10:18-19.) How have you seen this truth in your life?

JOURNAL

CHAPTER 7

GOD TALKS THROUGH DREAMS AND VISIONS

CHAPTER 4 FOCUSED ON THE HOLY SPIRIT. JESUS PROMISED TO send the Holy Spirit after He left the world physically, and He did just that at Pentecost. Acts chapter 2 records the events that happened on the day of Pentecost. After the Holy Spirit came down on the believers and they started to speak in other tongues or languages, Peter addressed the crowd. Peter quoted the Old Testament book of Joel, where Joel prophesied, "In the last days, God says, I will pour out My Spirit on all people. Your sons and daughters will prophesy, your young men will see visions, your old men will dream dreams. Even on my servants, both men and women, I will pour out my Spirit in those days, and they will prophesy" (Acts 2:17-18). (See also Joel 2:28-29.)

Peter said that this quote from Joel was being fulfilled at that very time, on that day of Pentecost. In the past, God's Spirit had only been available to a select few: prophets, kings, judges, and some religious leaders. Now, God's Spirit was made available to all believers. Not just to the "sons and daughters," but to the "servants" as well. They would see "visions" and they would dream "dreams," among other things.

God gave us the Bible to guide us and to help us get to know Him. He has also told us that He is unchanging (see Mal. 3:6). There are at least 200 references to dreams and visions in the Bible. Many events in the Bible are the fulfillment of these dreams and visions. Jesus Christ was even foretold to His earthly father through a dream in Matthew 1:20-21. To think that God would no longer use dreams and visions as a way to talk to, or communicate with us, is not logical. It would also be calling God a liar because He does not change. In the book of Numbers chapter 12, God talked about this very subject. "Listen to My words: 'When a prophet of the Lord is among you, I reveal Myself to him in visions, I speak to him in dreams. But this is not true of My servant Moses; he is faithful in all My house. With him I speak face to face, clearly and not in riddles; he sees the form of the Lord...'" (Num. 12:6-8). We have to remember that this quote comes from the beginning of the Bible, long before Jesus came and long before Pentecost. At this time, the only people that God was talking to through dreams and visions were the prophets. That changed after Pentecost when God sent the Holy Spirit to *all* believers.

God told us a lot about dreams and visions in this short passage from chapter 12 of Numbers. If we look at the original Hebrew and Greek texts used to write the Bible, we find that although there are at least nine different words used to say *dream*, we simply use the one word *dream* to cover them all.[1] We also find that there are at least 16 different words to describe a *vision*, but we simply use the one word *vision*, to describe all 16.[2] This tells us that there are many different types of dreams and visions. By using a Bible concordance, we find that there is somewhat of a pattern set up as to how these words are used and what the different variations consist of. God's own words, in chapter 12 of Numbers, seem to set up and follow this pattern.

God first said that He reveals Himself in visions. If we look up all 16 of the different words for *vision* and *visions* in Strong's Concordance, they could be collectively translated as: "to make known, to display or show clearly some information through a supernatural sight." A vision is a revelation that focuses on the visual. From this, we find that God uses a vision to reveal or show us something clearly or obviously through something we see. Sometimes a vision can be a symbolic picture, but it more often tends to be a literal picture. Many visions in the Bible happened while the person was awake, but some happened while the person was sleeping.

God also said that He speaks in dreams. Webster's dictionary defines *dream* as "a sequence of images, etc., passing through a sleeping person's mind." If we look up the nine different words used for *dream* and *dreams* in Strong's concordance, they could be collectively translated as "a supernatural revelation from God, disclosed through words or images." From this we find that God speaks to us through dreams but that the message will usually be changed into another form—into symbolic speech or imagery. The primary focus of a spiritual dream is God's communication with us, usually through symbolic images, but sometimes through words. A dream in the Bible always happens while the person is sleeping. Through my own experiences, and from what others have shared with me, I have found that it is a lot more common to have symbolic dreams than to have literal visions.

SYMBOLIC

Why does God speak to us most of the time in parables and riddles? Why does He usually give us dreams that are symbolic and not visions that are more literal? We are told in Numbers chapter 12 that God spoke clearly to Moses because he was the most humble man alive and because he was the most faithful out of all of God's people. The word *humble* means "submissive respect." *Faithful* means "loyal and worthy of trust." When I look at my life, I know that there have been more times than not when I have been anything but submissive, respectful, loyal to God, or worthy of His trust. According to God's Word, this explains why I (and most others) have had more dreams than visions and have had very few "close encounters" with the Lord like Moses did.

When we read the New Testament, we find that Jesus used many parables when speaking to people. A parable compares something familiar to the listener to something unfamiliar to the listener. It is symbolic. It helps a person understand a spiritual truth by comparing it to everyday items and events. This is the same principle that God uses when He gives us a spiritual dream or symbolic vision. Jesus's parables compelled those who were seeking spiritual truth to discover and understand the meaning of His parables. To other people, who were not receptive to the spiritual truth, or too stubborn, or too lazy, these parables were meaningless stories. This same principle applies to the spiritual dreams and symbolic visions that God gives us today. We are compelled to discover the meaning when we are seeking spiritual truth.

In Matthew 13:10-13, Jesus gives us more insight into this truth:

> *The disciples came to Him and asked, "Why do You speak to the people in parables?" He replied, "The knowledge of the secrets of the kingdom of heaven has been given to you, but not to them. Whoever has will be given more, and he will have an abundance. Whoever does not have, even what he has will be taken from him. This is why I speak to them in parables: Though seeing, they do not see; though hearing, they do not hear or understand."*

Jesus was saying that we all have the responsibility to make our own choices about Him based on what we have been told about Him or know about Him. The people who take what knowledge they have about Christ and believe in Him and seek Him will be given even more understanding and eternal life in Heaven. The people who reject Jesus after hearing about Him will also inherit eternal life, but it will be in hell with the devil.

UNDERSTANDING DREAMS AND VISIONS

When we become true believers in Christ, we have the Holy Spirit inside of us, and the Holy Spirit will give us understanding. This is true for our dreams and visions also! Let's look at how this applies to us today. Almost everyone has dreams. Some people have the ability to remember a lot of their dreams, while other people have not trained their minds to work in that way. Where do our dreams come from? What do they mean? If we believe what most people in the psychological field tell us, then God has no place in any of our dreams. But we know that the Bible says otherwise.

Once again, let's refer back to our angel and devil cartoon. This illustration also works for our dream life. Are you starting to see a pattern? Our dreams can come from God, from the devil, or from ourselves. The tricky part can be discerning which one of the three a dream came from. For instance, just because we have a "bad" dream doesn't mean that it didn't come from God. We read in Job 7:13-14, "When I think my bed will comfort me and my couch will ease my complaint, even then You frighten me with dreams and terrify me with visions." Job was saying that God can and does give us "bad" dreams sometimes. We read later, in Job 33:14-18:

> *For God does speak—now one way, now another—though man may not perceive it. In a dream, in a vision of the night, when deep sleep falls on men as they slumber in their beds, He may speak in their ears and terrify them with warnings, to turn man from wrongdoing and keep him from pride, to preserve his soul from the pit, his life from perishing by the sword.*

So we again find that God sometimes gives us bad dreams. These verses tell us that He uses these bad dreams as warnings. There are four reasons why God gives these warnings:

1. To turn a person from wrongdoing (sin).

2. To keep him from pride.

3. To preserve his soul from the pit (hell).

4. To preserve his life from perishing by the sword.

These reasons are self-explanatory. I can personally think of several dreams that I have had that were scary, but there is no doubt in my mind that they were warning dreams from God. I have also had other dreams that were not scary but were still warning dreams. Praise God that He loves and cares about us enough to talk to us and warn us in our dreams. Even Jesus's life was preserved through a warning dream. We read in Matthew chapter 2 that, after the "wise men" left the baby Jesus, God gave His earthly father, Joseph, a warning dream. He told him to take his family to Egypt because King Herod was going to try to kill the baby. Joseph listened to the dream and avoided the danger.

In my life, I have learned some serious lessons through warning dreams. Remember my story about crashing my motorcycle and severely injuring my shoulder? I told you that I had finally won an overall "A" class trophy at the final race of the previous year and that the very next time I rode my motorcycle, I got hurt. What I didn't tell you was that, before the race I that won, I had told a few different people that if I ever won an overall "A" trophy, I would quit racing. I had won several state championships in my class, but somehow an overall "A" win had eluded me. We were racing almost every weekend over a six state area, spending almost every extra penny that we had and skipping church a lot. I knew that God didn't want me spending all of this time and effort on something that was only for pleasure and pride.

The Bible tells us that God takes vows very seriously (see Num. 30:2). The spoken word is very powerful, even if it's spoken carelessly. When I won that overall "A" trophy but didn't quit racing, God took it seriously. After that race, but before I rode again, I started having nightmares about my racing. In my dreams, I would be riding and then fall into a bottomless hole, or things like that. The next time that I rode after my win was when I got hurt. God had warned me, but I refused to listen. Has that ever happened to you?

From my own experiences, from the stories that other people have shared with me, and from the research that I have done, I have reached the conclusion that we can use certain criteria to help us determine the origin of our dreams. First, if you are a Christian and you have a dream or vision from God, the Holy Spirit will often times help you to know it. That dream or vision will seem more real to you than life itself. It will stick in your memory, and you will often have trouble forgetting it, even if you want to. My first vision happened more than 30 years ago, and I can still shut my eyes and picture some of it. I have also found that almost every major dream and vision that I have had from God has had some living color in it. This is a big clue for me (although I and others I know have had informational or warning-type dreams that we know were from God that were devoid of any color). God talks to each of us differently, but we have to remember that God is consistent. You will often start to see patterns that He uses in your individual dreams.

Second, if God gives you a spiritual dream, and He doesn't give you the interpretation of the dream as it happens or right after it happens, it will trouble you. You will want to know what the dream meant. Joseph, in Genesis chapter 40-41, interpreted dreams for officials who were troubled by what they had dreamt. Each of them woke up, remembered their dream, and wanted to know what it meant. Later, when the pharaoh had two spiritual dreams, he also wanted to know what his dreams meant. This also is a good sign that the dream is from God—you will remember the dream clearly, and you will want to know its meaning.

The devil is very tricky, and it can be hard sometimes to distinguish the dreams that he sends our way. Once again, we have to rely on the Holy Spirit for discernment. All of the dreams that I have had from the devil have either started out in nearly black and white or ended up that way. If there is any color, it is dingy and shadowy at best. When dreams from the devil are over, they leave you feeling hopeless, abandoned, and unworthy of love. They don't just try to scare you into a change. They try to scare you into thinking that it's too late for you to get help, or that it's too late for you to change, or that you can't be helped because you're not worthy. I have had many dreams and visions from the devil where I dream that I am being tempted. Sometimes the temptation is about doing drugs, or sometimes it's about women. (The devil knows our weak areas!) Whatever the temptation may be, it's always something that I know is wrong.

In one particular dream, I was lying in my bed and a friend's wife walked up to the side of my bed wearing an untied bathrobe. I had always thought that this woman was very attractive, and in my dream she was holding out her hand to me. I told her that it wouldn't be right for us to come together because she was married and her husband was one of my friends. She never spoke, but continued to hold out her hand. I started to look at her body and then reached out and grabbed her hand to pull her into bed with me. When I grabbed her hand, it felt as cold as ice. I looked up at her, and her face had turned into a demonic face. It laughed hysterically, and I woke up. The worst part was that, after I woke up, I could still hear the demonic laughter for a while. This was obviously a dream from the devil.

This brings us to our last possibility for the origins of our dreams—ourselves. I'm sure that many of you can think of a time when you had a dream where some part of your body was not working right or hurt, and then you woke up to find that you were sleeping on that part of your body in a painful way. Or maybe you had some type of injury that was the cause of your dream. Maybe you dreamt that you had to go to the bathroom and then woke up because you really did have to go to the bathroom! These are all examples of dreams that come from within us. If we have some deep emotion or want that we are dealing with, it can cause us to have dreams. For instance, I have had many dreams in which I am trying to shoot a trophy buck or I find some antique motorcycle hidden away in a barn. This is because these are strong desires that I have stored away in my heart. Maybe we have a strong fear of something. This can cause us to have all sorts of dreams pertaining to that fear. This type of dream is usually forgotten fairly easily, and the origins are obvious to us. We know why we had them, and we typically understand what they were about.

KEEPING TRACK

As you know, I carried in my wallet a list of all the major things that God has done in my life and a list of my answered and unanswered prayers. I also kept track of my dreams and visions on that original document. When I started to write this book, I took the lists from my wallet and divided them into categories. Each chapter in this book represents a category—the ways God talks to me. As I started to write this chapter, I separated my dreams from my visions and made a list of each. The visions were easy to pick out because a vision is when God shows us something clearly through a supernatural sight, unlike the spiritual dreams that tend to be symbolic images.

Perhaps the most common form of a vision is something that most people have experienced and have no explanation for—*déjà vu*. The dictionary defines *déjà vu* as, "the illusion of having already experienced something actually being experienced for the first time." I rarely disagree with the dictionary, but in this case, I do. If you have ever had a *déjà vu* experience, you will agree with me that it is not an illusion—you actually did dream or pre-experience something. It is usually some small, insignificant thing that you often don't even remember until it occurs. The visions that I'm going to share with you are not *déjà vu* experiences; they are complete visions. But I think that God allows *déjà vu* experiences to happen so that we realize that our dreams have the ability to show us the future through the power of the Holy Spirit.

I told you about the vision that God gave me of my annual performance review the night before it happened. I had made up my mind that I was going to turn in my two-week notice if I didn't get what I wanted. God showed me exactly how the review was going to happen through a vision. It was clear, it was exact, and it was literal. After I woke up, the Holy Spirit told me not to be foolish but to be patient. If God would not have given me that vision and told me to be patient, I would have defiantly turned in my two-week notice that day, and I'm sure things would not have turned out as well for me as they did.

That vision happened while I was sleeping. But many visions occur while we are awake. Here is an example that happened some years ago. I came home late after work one night. I had stopped somewhere on the way home, and I had not only been smoking pot, but I had also been snorting cocaine. I was feeling horrible because I felt so guilty for what I had done. I went to bed and was praying for forgiveness. My body was feeling yucky, and I wanted to go to sleep, but I couldn't. I was praying to God, asking Him to help me and telling Him I was sorry. As I was praying, I saw a vision of some rolling hills with a quiet running stream going through them. It was a very peaceful scene. The grass looked soft and alive; the sun was shining. As I looked at the scene, I heard a gentle voice talking, quoting the 23rd Psalm. "The Lord is my shepherd, I shall not be in want. He makes me lie down in green pastures, He leads me beside quiet waters, He restores my soul...."

I know the vision was from God, and not the drugs or satan, because the voice—the Holy Spirit—spoke the entire Psalm and then asked me why I continued to choose the bad feelings that drugs bring, instead of choosing the peace that God provides. Every time I remember this vision, I cry. God is so merciful! He never gives up on us. I'm positive that this is the reason why He chose me to write this book—to show that no one is too bad, too far gone, or too stubborn to receive His love. The next day when I woke up, God confirmed His message to me—the Bible reading for my devotion that day was the 23rd Psalm. What I had seen the night before was no drug-induced trance but a vision from God. He showed me what true peace looked like in a picture, and He had the perfect words describe it.

Another example of a vision happened in relation to the writing of this book. A few years ago, when God started making it clear that He wanted me to write this book, I told Him that He was going to have to pull this whole thing off because I didn't have a clue about any of it. The Holy Spirit has faithfully inspired me throughout this project. I asked Him about the title, and He responded instantly. I have found that my job is to listen and then try to write what He tells me. At the beginning of this project, I wrongly assumed that, as the author, I would be responsible for the book cover design. This troubled me because I am not an artist. I prayed regularly about the issue during the first few weeks of writing and then stopped when I received no answer. Although I had stopped praying about it, I was still troubled.

A week later, while praying about a completely different subject, the Lord gave me a clear vision of a cover design that represented what this book is about. I got up from prayer and sketched it as He explained what it meant. The word *God* was in red to show His power and represent the atoning blood of Jesus. Three red arrows were going into an ear representing the Father, the Son, and the Holy Spirit. The cover was white and the words were black, representing plain truth. The ear was outlined with no color to show that all people of every race are accepted and considered equal. Although due to the accident this isn't the design we used, the vision quieted my unrest about the cover and helped me to move forward and focus on writing the book.

REMEMBRANCES

The first vision I ever had happened more than 30 years ago, while I was sleeping. It happened shortly after Jesus hugged me. I can still shut my eyes and see parts of it. I had a vision of myself, walking with Jesus in Heaven. I remember that the walls were made of the most beautiful stones imaginable. I knew this was Heaven and that I was walking with God. The only explanation for this knowledge is that the Holy Spirit told me. Anyone who truly knows me can tell you that I have always had a fascination with rocks and stones. I think that this vision, at the age of five, caused that interest. There is a description of Heaven in the Bible that talks about the walls being made out of precious stones. (See Revelation 21.) Only the Holy Spirit could have shown me Heaven through this vision.

Years later, I had two visions that essentially led me to begin the list of visions that I keep in my wallet (though they were not about keeping a list). I had been talking to some friends about the existence of God. These friends were a married couple with whom my wife and I spent a lot of time when we first got married. These two visions that I had were actually about them, and it's because of what happened with those visions that, after our conversation, I started the list. Lori and I had decided that we were going to start trying to have children after a few years of marriage. We had a miscarriage first, and then we had a tubular pregnancy that ended with an emergency operation. After some months, Lori became pregnant again, yet we waited to tell anyone because of the previous two tragic experiences.

One week, I had to attend training in another town, and it happened to be the town where the husband of this couple worked. I told him that I would meet him for lunch on one of the days that I was there. I planned on telling him that Lori was pregnant again when we met for lunch. The night before I was to meet him, I had a vision of him and his wife at a doctor's office, where she was about to get an abortion. The next day, when I told him that Lori was pregnant, he told me that his wife had missed her period that month but that they didn't know for sure if she was pregnant. I immediately thought about my dream and told him that, if she was pregnant, I was happy for them. He said that he hoped she wasn't pregnant because it would not be good timing for them. She was working full-time at an excellent job and was going to night school also. We dropped the subject and didn't talk about it again. I never even told Lori about the dream I had.

Sometime later, after we brought home our new baby, they dropped by unexpectedly to visit us. We were sitting around, talking about the baby, and Lori said that she didn't know how anybody could ever have an abortion. The couple became uneasy and said that they wanted to go get some cigarettes. They asked if I wanted to go along to check out their new truck and told me I could drive it. Lori stayed home with the child.

When we got in the truck, the wife turned to me and said that they were "those" kind of people, referring to Lori's remark. My mind was racing. I realized that God had shown me what was going to happen through my vision and that I had failed miserably by not saying anything when I was given the chance. I felt so guilty and horrible that I couldn't say anything at all. I started the truck and acted as if she hadn't said a word. We drove away in silence, and after that night, we rarely saw each other. Not only had I failed the first time, but I also failed a second time by trying to pretend that it hadn't happened.

I wish I would have told them the truth about my vision, but it seemed too late. At least I could have shared the love and forgiveness of God with them, but instead I was silent, which made it worse for them. I hope you understand an important reality that this book continues to prove. God consistently tries to use us—everyday people—to do His work, but we must be willing to listen and obey.

After some time, I had a dream (or vision) in which I was talking with this same couple about God. In my dream, the Holy Spirit told me to start at the very beginning when I talked to them about God. It had been months since we had seen them, but the very next day they called and asked if we could get together. I knew it was no coincidence. After what had happened the last time, God had given me another vision about them, and I was determined to be obedient. They came to our house that night, and we had a few drinks and some casual conversation. I didn't want to "weird them out" or make them feel uncomfortable right away, so I waited for the right opportunity to start talking about God. I realized it was getting late and that, if I didn't bring up the subject soon, I wasn't going to get the chance. I finally started the "God" conversation and began with Adam and Eve, because in my vision the Holy Spirit had told me to start at the beginning. As soon as I started talking, the wife said that she couldn't believe what a "coincidence" this was because just the night before, they had had a discussion with somebody else about the validity of Adam and Eve.

She had just graduated from night school and had taken a "religion" class where the teacher had taught the class that the Bible was a bunch of fictional stories. After a short discussion, I realized that I had no way to prove to them that Adam and Eve were real people. I told them that, even if I couldn't prove that Adam and Eve were real, I had no other choice but to believe in God because of all the things that He had done in my life. They wanted to know what kind of stuff I was talking about. I tried to think of all the things that I knew God had done for me, but because of the drinking and drugs, I couldn't think of much, and the few things that I could think of, I wasn't comfortable sharing with them.

When they left that night, I knew that I had failed my mission, again. Two times God had wanted me to reach out to this couple for Him, and two times I failed miserably. The next morning, I wrote down everything that God had done in my life that I could remember. I carried the list in my wallet so that, when I remembered something else, or when a new thing happened, I could record it. I never wanted to be put in another situation where I couldn't recall what God had done for me, even if I had to use a list.

The Bible tells us that God will make good come out of bad for the people who love Him. I failed to do what God wanted me to with this couple, but God used those failures to lead me to create my list and eventually this book. Praise God for His patience and mercy! What failures have you had that God is waiting to use for His plan and His glory?

ADDICTION

Remember when I told you that I had some prayers on my unanswered list that were there because God made me wait several years before He answered them? Well one prayer was about my addiction to illegal drugs and alcohol. I tried to quit doing drugs more times than I can count. I prayed about it, and I had other people pray about it, but it never seemed to change anything. I would throw my stuff away, but before long, I was getting more or going somewhere that I could get high. If I was able to stay sober, I was irritable and miserable— just ask my wife. I might have been able to make it for five or six days, but by the end of that time, I was ready to snap. This went on for many before God finally helped me stop. It didn't stop overnight, but gradually, my desire diminished. When I had done everything that I could to quit, God showed up and took my addiction away. More about that later.

If you can relate, if you know what it's like to have an area of sin in your life that has become a stronghold, please know that it can be stopped. Maybe you think that, if God talks to you and tells you to quit whatever it is you are doing, you can. Well maybe, but it didn't work that way for someone as stubborn as me. Remember when God called my name in the church? The only two other times when God has spoken out loud to me, through my ears, were also concerning drugs. So maybe you're asking yourself what this has to do with dreams and visions. Well, let me tell you.

For the first ten years of our marriage, I had a recurring dream about Lori. I had these dreams at least a few times a month. The situations were always different, but the story was the same. We would be someplace or another and she would end up cheating on me, right in front of me. She never seemed to care that I was there, watching it happen. I always reacted the same way in my dreams, and after I would start out feeling bad and crying, trying to talk her out of it, but it never worked. Finally I would get angry and tell her that if that's what she wanted, she could just leave.

The dreams were so real that, when I woke up, I had a hard time separating the dream from reality for a while. She could always tell when I had one of "those" dreams because I would be cold and distant in the morning. She had never done anything in our relationship to make me think that she would do this sort of thing, but I continued to have these nightmares, in spite of her reassurances.

This one particular night, I dreamt that a van pulled up to our house and a man got out with a duffle bag. It was an old boyfriend of hers. I looked out the window and asked Lori what he was doing at our house. She told me that he was going to spend the night. I asked her where he was going to stay, and she said in our bed. I pleaded with her as he knocked on the door. I kept telling her how much I loved her and how bad this was making me feel. She had a puzzled look on her face and asked, "Why?"

I told her that it was going to make me feel bad because of how much I loved her. I could tell by the look on her face that, as always, she just didn't understand. Usually in these dreams, I had to sit and watch her cheat on me, but this time, I woke up. My pillow and face were wet with tears as I sat there in the dark, looking at her sleeping next to me. I repeated out loud the last thing I had said to her in my dream, "Why can't you understand how much I love you?"

For the second time in my life, God spoke out loud to me; He turned my question to Lori back at me. He asked me, "Why don't you understand how much I love you?" There was no question in my mind who was talking to me, and I said, "What do you mean, God?" He repeated the question to me again, and again I asked Him what He meant. God told me that every time I used drugs or drank alcohol or did anything else to get the peace and fulfillment that I wanted, I was cheating on Him. He said that, not only was I cheating on Him, but I also did it in front of Him, with full knowledge that He could see me. That's all He said, and there was nothing else that I could say. I felt sick to my stomach as I realized that these dreams that I had been having for the last ten years were actually about me and my relationship with God.

It was about 3:30 in the morning when this happened, and I got out of bed and opened my Bible. I started reading where God compares Himself to a groom and the Body of believers to a bride. I knew that this was no coincidence, and it made me hurt so badly that I fell to the floor and sobbed for a long time. I haven't had another dream about Lori cheating on me since that night. I wish I could say that I never did drugs again, but I can't. If ever there was a person who had every reason not to fall back into a particular sin, it would be me. I used to think about how stupid and hard-headed the Israelites were when they were in the desert for those 40 years. God provided many miracles for them, but they kept falling back into their old sins. If I had been part of that group, God probably would have kept us out there for 80 years! (I want you to know that it is not easy to write these stories down and share them. Please understand that I am writing this book out of obedience and not in search of attention. I know that God is going to use it to help people get closer to Him. Looking honestly at yourself can be painful, but the fruit of it far outweighs the cost.)

I had many other dreams when God talked to me about my drug addiction. One that was particularly vivid still sticks in my mind. In the dream, I was walking down a road, and I started to limp. I realized that there was something wrong with my right leg and that it was hindering my journey. I looked at my leg and saw that there was a tick stuck in the back of it. It was white and enlarged, indicating that it had been there for a long time. My leg was very swollen and sore.

I pulled the tick off and started to squeeze out the pus from my leg. What seemed like gallons of pus poured out of my leg. One of my friends appeared and said how gross and disgusting it was. I kept squeezing, but I began to realize that I couldn't get it all out. Another pair of hands appeared and helped me get the rest out, and I continued walking down the road, now with no problem.

When I woke up from that dream, I knew exactly what it meant because the Holy Spirit had given me the interpretation. The tick stood for my drug addiction. It had been there long enough that it started to severely hinder my walk with God. The pus in my leg stood for the effects of the drug addiction on my life. My friend who told me how gross it was actually was another drug user, but he did drugs "socially" and wasn't addicted. The other pair of hands with no body represented the Holy Spirit, who was going to help me completely remove the addiction from my life, after I made the initial effort. The easy walk after the removal of the tick and the pus showed me that, once I got past this problem, my walk with God would be unhindered.

I had another short dream, which actually occurred several times, that was also about my drug addiction. In my dream I knew that my body needed a "valve adjustment." This is something that I did to engines quite regularly in my job. In my dream, I would get out all of my normal tools and then realize that I didn't know the location of the adjusters or how to perform the repair. I would look at my body and get upset when I realized that I couldn't do the repair myself. God was telling me that I needed to make some adjustments but that I couldn't do them by myself—I needed His help.

Almost exactly one year after I had my last dream about Lori cheating on me, I had another dream that was similar. I dreamt that we were at a big gathering of people and that there was an attractive man there who motioned for Lori to come by him. Music was playing, and people were dancing. She went to him, and they danced very closely for a brief moment before she came back to stand by me. I told her that I didn't like what she had done. She reasoned that they had only danced together, that it was just a short dance, and that she had then come right back to me. When I woke up, I knew that this dream was not about Lori; it was about my relationship with God again.

I quickly got out of bed and headed for the bathroom, as if I could avoid what I knew was coming. I had only taken about two steps when I heard God speak to me. It was the third time in my life that I had ever heard him with my ears, and it was also the last, so far. He said, "I the Lord your God am a jealous God!" I didn't have to ask Him what He meant this time because I knew. By this point in my life, God had already taken away my addiction to drugs. I no longer craved drugs or felt as if I couldn't live without them, but every so often, I would still get high or drunk. I knew that it wasn't right, but I told myself that, compared to the way that I used to live, I was doing great. God let me know through this dream that even these small infrequent "dances" with drugs made Him jealous.

FREEDOM FIGHTING

As I look through my list, I notice dreams that can be grouped as fighting or combat dreams. When talking to others about their dreams, I have found that it is common for Christians to have this type of dream. They can vary greatly in background, but they all have one thing in common—fighting against some type of enemy. You are usually outnumbered and out-gunned. If you have a weapon, it rarely operates, and if it does work, it's ineffective. I can remember having this type of dream ever since I was a small child. Either I or my family was being attacked. Very often, the dream took place in a war setting, but not always. I continue to have these dreams, and now my children are experiencing these dreams also.

Many times, these dreams are symbolic of the spiritual warfare that we are going through in our day-to-day lives. They are scary because they are real in a sense. The devil and his demons are fighting against us and God. I will explain this further in the last chapter, but it has been my experience that sometimes, when we are having these dreams, the demons are right there causing them. I spent the majority of my life terrified of these dreams, but not anymore. After more than 30 years of dealing with the fear that comes with these dreams, I have finally understood how to overcome it by the power of the Holy Spirit.

One particular night, I was awakened several times by noises in our house. I felt the presence of evil, and it scared me. Each time that I fell asleep, I would find myself in various forms of warfare dreams—then a noise in the house would startle me awake again. Our family dog heard the noises too, and she kept growling. I told the demonic presence to leave our home in the name of Jesus, but because I was so scared, they kept coming back, feeding off of my fear and lack of faith. I prayed to God feverishly, pleading with Him to deal with these spirits that were plaguing me. I still had my hands folded when I fell into another one of these dreams, but this one was different. I could see myself in bed sleeping. There was a noise in my dream that woke me up, so I got out of bed, and my dog and I searched the house but found nothing.

The dog whined to go outside, so I opened the door and stood out on the step to wait for her. She went to the corner of the house and started growling. I walked to where she was and saw a big black cat the size of a cougar or mountain lion. It charged at us out of the darkness and chased us to the steps. Our backs were against the wall, and we were trapped. I started to get a righteous anger that this huge cat was on my property and was trying to attack me and my dog.

All of a sudden, someone I couldn't see handed me a large wooden shaft or rod. It was about three to four inches round and about four feet long. I knew this rod was to be used as a weapon. I chased the cat down, and as I was chasing it, the cat got smaller. When I finally caught the cat, it was a normal-sized house cat, and I crushed his head quite easily with the wooden rod. I looked around and there were more cats that I hadn't seen before. I killed all of the cats by crushing their heads with this large rod. I went back into the house, satisfied that it was so simple, and I went back to bed.

I woke up when the dream was over, with my hands still folded from praying. I felt no presence of evil and absolutely no fear. The Holy Spirit told me that I didn't have to tolerate or fear being attacked because He would give me the tools and power that I needed to fight the enemy. As we are told in Psalm 23:4, "Even though I walk through the valley of the shadow of death, I will fear no evil, for You are with me; Your rod and Your staff, they comfort me." I realized that the large wooden shaft that I was handed was an extra large shepherd's staff—a multi-purpose tool that shepherds use as a weapon when needed. Our Lord is the Good Shepherd, and He protects us with His weapons, which are extra big!

It was also significant that the shepherd's rod was used to "crush" the heads of the cats. God told the snake (satan) in Genesis 3:15 that his head would be crushed. He was foretelling what would happen when Jesus died and rose again—satan would be defeated forever. Psalm 68:21 says, "Surely God will crush the heads of His enemies...." In both verses, we find the same thought—God crushing the heads of His enemies. For 30 years, I had tried to fight the enemy on my own and had even asked God more than once to do it for me. This dream showed me that God doesn't always fight for us. Sometimes He empowers us through the Holy Spirit to fight and defeat the enemy (see Rom. 16:20). Now, when I have a combative dream, it doesn't scare me. I don't rely on myself. I let the Holy Spirit work through me to declare victory over the enemy.

INTERPRETATION

This brings us to another very important job of the Holy Spirit—interpretation. A lot of people have spiritual dreams, but without the Holy Spirit's interpretation, dreams are just meaningless stories. This is what happened when non-believers heard Jesus's parables. They were just meaningless stories to them. The Bible tells us very clearly, in at least two different passages, that without the help of God, our dreams can't be interpreted. As in the story of Joseph, with the help of God, he interpreted two people's dreams, plus the pharaoh's dreams. In Genesis 40:8, Joseph said, "Do not interpretations belong to God?" He knew that God had given him the meaning of the dreams, and he gave God the credit.

If you have had a dream that bothers you, pray to God and ask Him for the interpretation. I can't find anywhere in the Bible where God promises to give us an interpretation, but I do know that, if we want an interpretation, it has to come from Him. He might use someone else to give us the meaning, but it still comes from Him. Sometimes God gives the interpretation of a dream as it is happening. Sometimes He will reveal the meaning as soon as the dream is over. Other times it can take several years before we know the meaning of a dream. In Joseph's story, it took several years before his dreams about his family bowing to him were actually fulfilled. We shouldn't doubt the validity or the importance of our dreams just because they don't materialize right away or make sense to us. The dreams that I had about my wife cheating on me are good examples of this. It took more than ten years before God told me what those dreams really meant.

When God gives you a spiritual dream and doesn't give you the interpretation right away, it will haunt you. We read in Daniel chapters 2 and 4 that King Nebuchadnezzar had two different dreams that bothered him. The king asked all those around him to interpret his dream, but no one could. Daniel told the king, "No wise man, enchanter, magician or diviner can explain to the king the mystery he has asked about, but there is a God in heaven who reveals mysteries..." (Dan. 2:27-28). God gave Daniel the interpretation of the king's dreams, but Daniel gave God all the credit. Like King Nebuchadnezzar, we too should search for the meaning of our dreams. When I started writing this chapter, and I looked over all of the dreams that I have kept track of, I realized that there were a handful for which God had not yet revealed the meaning. I didn't think I should write about something that I didn't understand myself, so I decided to pray for the meaning of these dreams before continuing to write.

I prayed and I read the Bible, and I prayed some more and I read the Bible some more. After several days, I was starting to get a little impatient. I wasn't making any progress on the book, and I didn't feel any closer to the answers that I was looking for. I decided to pray and fast until God gave me the answers that I was looking for. I can be a little stubborn sometimes. I continued to read the Bible and pray from very early in the morning to very late at night. After a few days, He started giving me the answers that I was searching for, plus more. I filled eight pages of notebook paper with the information that God gave me. I could feel that He was enjoying our interaction—He was happy that I was submerging myself in His presence and searching Him out. Our time together reminded me of a woman who plays hard to get so she can test the love of her suitor. I realized that I, too, was enjoying this time together.

I finally came to a place where I felt like God had answered my questions as much as He was going to. He gave me the meaning of most of my dreams, as well as the confidence that I needed to move forward. I knelt in prayer and thanked Him for being patient with a stubborn joker like myself. During this prayer, I asked Him one more time for the interpretation of a dream that I had had years earlier. As I was praying, He made me remember a dream that wasn't even on my list. This dream was similar to the dream in question, but not exactly the same. After He recounted this dream to me, He gave me its meaning and several pertinent Bible passages.

Here is the dream: I was at home, working in the garage. Several vans pulled into my driveway, and people in blue T-shirts emerged. They were part of a church group, and they asked me if I would join them in their projects. I asked them about the projects before I committed myself. They took me to a house that they were fixing up for one of the church members and showed me all of the work that they had already done. The front door was sagging because the frame was dropping, so they had nailed two-by-fours to the exterior of the house in order to try to solve the problem. The windows and walls were also crooked and drooping, and they had nailed boards to the exterior of the house in those areas too.

I inspected the house and found that the foundation was completely gone below the door and rotted in several other places. In some areas, there were holes large enough for a man to walk through. The foundation was made out of bricks in a few places, but the mortar holding the bricks together was also rotten and crumbling. The cement portions of the basement were so rotted that I could put my fingers right through them. I called the leader over and asked him why they had neglected to fix the real problems of the house. He acknowledged that the problems were there, but he said that it would cost too much and take too long to fix the foundation. I argued with him that the repairs that they had made were only temporary fixes at best. He again told me that they weren't going to fix the foundation because it would take too long and cost too much.

After God recalled this dream for me, He told me what it meant. He said that the large group of people in blue T-shirts represented the majority of church people today. It was not only church members but also their leaders. He said that the house represented the lives of everyday people. The problems of the house were the problems that these people had in their lives—common everyday problems such as divorce and financial issues, as well as depression, anxiety, anger, and rejection. The patch jobs that they were doing stood for the way that people often handle these problems.

CHANGED LIVES

Instead of dealing with the real issue, the foundation, many people fix only the symptoms with useless patches. Patches that people, in their own power, use to solve their problems include illegal drugs, alcohol, shopping, and even doctor-prescribed drugs. Some people patch their problems through a constant search for pleasure, entertainment, or financial success, instead of dealing with the root cause of their inner unrest and personal turmoil. Other patches involve hollow rituals and meaningless religious traditions. The list includes anything that we do or use to try to fix our problems apart from the Lord. Without complete submission to God, our foundation will never be Rock solid.

God showed me that the foundation represented our relationship with Him—Father, Son, and Holy Spirit. He said that many people knew things about who He was, but they didn't really know Him. The bricks represented solid facts about Him, but if there was nothing to bind those facts together, they were of no value. Without a true relationship with God, knowing facts about Him is not going to save us. Our relationship with Him begins with faith, which leads to active obedience. Our faith in Jesus brings salvation, and active obedience is not a substitution for our faith, but a verification of it. God was not telling me that we can earn our salvation. Rather, He was saying that, if we have true faith in Him, our lives will change. A solid foundation, or relationship with Him, is based on faith that leads to submission.

We read in Second Timothy 2:19, "Nevertheless, God's solid foundation stands firm, sealed with this inscription: 'The Lord knows those who are His,' and, 'Everyone who confesses the name of the Lord must turn away from wickedness.'" Here the Bible tells us that true faith in God results in changed behavior. We read what Jesus had to say about this subject in the following verses:

> *Not everyone who says to Me, "Lord, Lord," will enter the kingdom of heaven, but only he who does the will of My Father who is in heaven. Many will say to Me on that day, "Lord, Lord, did we not prophesy in Your name, and in Your name drive out demons and perform many miracles?" Then I will tell them plainly, "I never knew you. Away from Me, you evildoers!" Therefore everyone who hears these words of Mine and puts them into practice is like a wise man who built his house on the rock. The rain came down, the streams rose, and the winds blew and beat against that house; yet it did not fall, because it had its foundation on*

the rock. But everyone who hears these words of Mine and does not put them into practice is like a foolish man who built his house on sand. The rain came down, the steams rose, and the winds blew and beat against that house, and it fell with a great crash (Matthew 7:21-27).

Jesus made some pretty strong points in this passage. He said that not everyone who calls Him "Lord" will enter Heaven, but only the people who also do God's will. The Lord also says that, after a person hears His message, he has a strong foundation only if he puts His words into practice. To build on the Rock, we have to be hearing, responding disciples. This relationship with Him starts with our acceptance of Him as Savior and Lord, and then leads to our obedience to Him. People who build their houses on the sand build their lives on something other than a strong relationship with God. It could be wealth, success, pleasure, health, popularity, or other people. All of these things will let us down in the end, and none of them can secure for us an eternal place in Heaven like Jesus can. My addiction to illegal drugs and alcohol kept me from building a Rock solid foundation on Him—thankfully, I have been delivered from that quicksand.

Going back to my dream, it becomes apparent why the church group's leader didn't want to take the time or pay the costs associated with constructing a solid foundation. True relationships take a lot of time! For example, a good marriage is a life-long commitment, 24 hours a day, 7 days a week, 365 days a year. A real relationship with God is a daily walk with Him, not a Sunday morning jog or a ten-minute-a-day run. In order to give this relationship the time that it needs and deserves, most people need to remove other things from their schedules. This is the high cost of constructing a Rock solid foundation. Jesus asks us to turn every area of our lives over to Him. This includes control over our time, career, finances, other relationships, friends, and pleasures. It might cost us persecution, loss of social status, and, in some cases, even death.

This is what Jesus was talking about in Luke 14:33, "In the same way, any of you who does not give up everything he has cannot be My disciple." This might sound scary, but Jesus also gave us these reassuring words in Matthew 11:28-30. "Come to Me, all you who are weary and burdened, and I will give you rest. Take My yoke upon you and learn from Me, for I am gentle and humble in heart, and you will find rest for your souls. For My yoke is easy and My burden is light." What more reassuring words could our Savior possibly give us?

I realize that it may seem like we veered away from dreams and visions a little, but this lengthy interpretation of this last dream is critical. God showed me that this entire book could be summed up in this one dream. The book focuses on different ways that God talks to us, but when looked at as a whole, these different types of communication are also a complete picture of what a healthy relationship with God can involve. God wants our relationship with Him to cover every area of our lives and be the foundation that keeps us solid!

MAKING YOUR OWN LIST

I could share with you many more dreams and visions that God has given me, but this sampling proves that God can and does talk to everyday people through dreams and visions. I encourage you to write down all of the dreams that you can remember. Don't forget that sometimes we won't remember a dream until later. That's OK. Add to the list as you have more dreams, and you will see patterns emerge. This ongoing list will be your very own dream vocabulary. You will see how God tailors dreams especially for you.

Keep in mind that, very often, God gives us different dreams that mean the same thing. It is His way of telling us something in more than one way. We saw this happen in the story of Joseph's interpretation of

Pharaoh's dreams; he had two different dreams that meant the same thing. I have found that God has done this for me many times as well; I receive different dreams with the same meaning. Until God gives us the interpretation, we might not even realize that the dreams are related!

You may want to keep a notebook near your bed, like I do, so that you can write about your dreams before you forget them. If you are not used to remembering your dreams, it may take you some time, but practice will help. Some people have more dreams than others, but don't be discouraged. When you have a spiritual dream, ask God to give you the interpretation through His Holy Spirit. This is the part that will turn your dreams into helpful tools. God talks through dreams and visions!

YOUR TURN

Write about all of the visions that God has given you. Remember that a vision is something that He shows us clearly through a supernatural window or sight. You may have been asleep or awake. It could be something that has already come to pass, such as my annual performance review, or it might be something that hasn't happened yet, such as my dream about Heaven.

Write about the spiritual dreams God has given you. Spiritual dreams are dreams that you have no problem remembering—they might not make sense on the surface, but you remember them and wonder what they meant. Very often you can recall the exact color of an object in the dream. They are usually symbolic, like Jesus's parables. The Holy Spirit may have already told you what they mean, or maybe not.

_____

_____

_____

_____

_____

_____

_____

_____

_____

_____

STUDY QUESTIONS

1. On the day of Pentecost, Peter explained what was happening by referring to a prophecy from Joel 2:28-29 (see Acts 2:17-18). What was God doing differently with the Holy Spirit starting at that time and why is that important for believers today?

2. The Bible has over two hundred references to dreams and visions. In Numbers 12:6, God talks about dreams and visions.

   a) What did the book text give as a definition for a dream?

   b) What did the book text give as a definition for a vision?

c) One tends to be more symbolic while the other tends to be more literal. Which is which and why is that important to know?

3. Why does God often speak to us through symbolism? (See Numbers 12:7-8.) What characteristic set Moses apart and caused God to speak to him face to face?

4. What is a parable? Why did Jesus choose to teach with parables? (See Matthew 13:10-13.)

5. What three sources can our dreams and visions come from? (Think about the cartoon analogy.)

   ▪ a.

   ▪ b.

   ▪ c.

6. Can God give us bad dreams, or nightmares? (See Job 7:13-14; 33:14-18.) What are four purposes God might have for giving us frightening dreams?

   ▪ a.

   ▪ b.

   ▪ c.

   ▪ d.

7. How can our dreams and visions be interpreted? (See Genesis 40:8; Daniel 2:27-28.)

ENDNOTES

1. *Strong's NIV Exhaustive Concordance*, s.v. "Dream," "Dreams."
2. *Strong's NIV Exhaustive Concordance*, s.v. "Vision," "Visions."

JOURNAL

CHAPTER 8

GOD TALKS THROUGH ANGELS

MUCH HAS BEEN SAID AND WRITTEN ABOUT ANGELS—SOME FAC-
tual and some fictional. There are nearly 300 references to angels in
the Bible—that is fact. According to Webster's dictionary, *angel* means
"messenger of God." An angel is a spiritual being created by God, for
God. As Paul wrote, "For by Him all things were created: things in
heaven and on earth, visible and invisible, whether thrones or powers
or rulers or authorities; all things were created by Him and for Him"
(Col. 1:16). Angels are also powerful servants of God who obey Him.
The psalmist wrote, "Praise the Lord, you His angels, you mighty
ones who do His bidding, who obey His word" (Ps. 103:20). Hebrews
further explains that angels are sent by God to do His will. "...He
makes His angels winds, His servants flames of fire" (Heb. 1:7).

Later in that same chapter, the writer of Hebrews said, "Are not
all angels ministering spirits sent to serve those who will inherit
salvation?" (Heb. 1:14). Here God tells us the main purpose for
sending His angels to earth: to help and minister to His true believers.
According to Webster's dictionary, *minister* means "one who serves as

an agent for another." In its verb form, it means "to give help to." So we find that angels are agents of God, sent by Him to attend to His people. Psalm 34:7 builds on this same theme, "The angel of the Lord encamps around those who fear Him, and He delivers them." Again, we find that God sends His angels to attend to His believers. How comforting to know that, even though we don't usually see the angels that God has sent for us, they are here and ready to help us in unseen ways.

An excellent example of this is in the book of Second Kings chapter 6 when the prophet Elisha kept warning the king of Israel about the enemy's location. God told Elisha where the enemy camps were, and then Elisha would tell the king of Israel. The king of Aram found out what was happening and sent men to capture Elisha so that he wouldn't interfere in the war again. The enemy king "sent horses and chariots and a strong force" to Dothan, where Elisha was staying. The story continues:

> *They went by night and surrounded the city. When the servant of the man of God [Elisha] got up and went out early the next morning, an army with horses and chariots had surrounded the city. "Oh, my lord, what shall we do?" the servant asked. "Don't be afraid," the prophet answered. "Those who are with us are more than those who are with them." And Elisha prayed, "O Lord, open his eyes so he may see." Then the Lord opened the servant's eyes, and he looked and saw the hills full of horses and chariots of fire all around Elisha. As the enemy came down toward him, Elisha prayed to the Lord, "Strike these people with blindness." So He struck them with blindness, as Elisha had asked* (2 Kings 6:14-18).

This account gives us a vivid picture of the unseen reality of our lives. If Elisha had not prayed to God to open his servant's eyes, the man would not have seen all of the angels that were there to protect them. We have to remember that God and His ways are constant, unchanging. He sent angels to do His work in the Bible, and He continues to use angels to do His will today—right now.

UNAWARE

I wonder how many times angels have been attending to us when we didn't see them. If we believe in God and believe His Word, the Bible, we have to believe that what He tells us is true. God uses angels to help us get through life! He talks to us through this angelic activity as a way to show us how much He loves us. At the beginning of this book, you read how the Lord sent two angels to save my life when the truck fell on me. While my spirit was separated from my body and floating up in the ceiling, I was able to see the angels perfectly. As soon as my spirit had rejoined my body and I was looking through my human eyes, I could no longer see the angels. This is just like the previous story from Second Kings. The Lord sends His angels, but we often can't see them with our human eyes.

The Bible tells us that sometimes God sends angels and we can't tell them apart from ordinary people. "Do not forget to entertain strangers, for by so doing some people have entertained angels without knowing it" (Heb. 13:2). Abraham experienced this when he gave food and shelter to three strangers who showed up one day. He soon found out that two of the visitors were angels and the third "person" was the Lord Himself (see Gen. 18). From these examples, we can see that sometimes angels look like normal people, as can the Lord. When God appears in human form in the Bible, the phrase "the angel of the Lord" is used to describe Him. Even though God is a Spirit, He sometimes chooses to deliver His messages Himself in the visible form of a person. The Bible typically refers to the messenger as "the angel of the Lord." In these cases, the context of what is said commonly shows that it is the Lord who is speaking, not an angel. Examples of this include Genesis 22:15-18 and Judges 6:21-23.

I went to college with a guy who said he was sure that an angel had introduced him to his wife because there was no other possible explanation. He had been visiting a town quite some distance from his home, where his wife-to-be was also visiting. They were both separately at a large outing in a crowd of people. A person he didn't know introduced him, by name, to his wife-to-be. He thought this person was someone that his friend knew. His wife-to-be thought the same thing because, although she didn't know the person, he introduced her by name too. These two were from two separate groups, from opposite areas of the state, and they had never met before. But the stranger introduced them and then disappeared before anyone could find out who he was. This man ended up dating the woman and eventually married her, all because the stranger had introduced them. God uses angels.

GUARDIAN ANGELS

One important function of angels is as guardian angels. Jesus told us in Matthew 18:10, "See that you do not look down on one of these little ones. For I tell you that their angels in heaven always see the face of My Father in heaven." This verse shows us not only that God highly values children but also that their guardian angels are given direct access to God at all times. This versecould explain why I had such a dramatic experience with God at the age of five. When I prayed for Jesus to hold me and comfort me, I received an immediate answer to my prayer. Not only was I held and comforted, but I was also given complete peace.

This point is exampled in Genesis chapter 21. Abraham sent his maidservant, Hagar, and the child that she had by him into the wilderness at the request of his wife. The boy was about 13 years of age. The woman and her son were in the desert and had run out of water. She put the boy under some bushes and went a short distance away because she thought that he was going to die, and she didn't want to see it happen. She and the boy were crying when the angel of God called to her from Heaven and told her not to fear. He said that God heard the boy crying there under the bushes. It goes on to say that God opened her eyes and that she was shown a well with water, which saved their lives. The angel made a point of saying that God heard the boy crying. It is also clear that God took action right away. I believe it was because his guardian angel brought his prayers to God's immediate attention. The angel of God then told the mother what to do and not to fear.

ANGEL ENCOUNTERS

During my research of angels in the Bible, I discovered that all of the angel encounters can be separated into seven categories—seven different ways in which angels accomplish God's will.

The first and most common angel task is delivering God's messages to people. God used angels to be His spokesmen in Genesis chapter 18 to tell Abraham and Sarah that they would have a child. When God tested Abraham with the task of sacrificing his only son, it was the angel of the Lord who stopped Abraham. In the Old Testament, there are several more examples of God using angels as messengers. At the beginning of the New Testament, we find angels telling Mary and Joseph that they were going to have Jesus as their child (see Luke 1). Angels also announced Jesus's birth to the shepherds who were watching their flocks in the fields near Bethlehem (see Luke 2). After Jesus was crucified and buried, an angel announced His resurrection (see Matt. 28). When Jesus ascended into Heaven, two angels announced that Jesus would return someday just like He left, in the clouds (see Acts 1:10-11).

These are just a few examples of the many times in the Bible that God used angels to deliver His message.

The second angel task is protecting God's people. In the Old Testament book of Daniel, chapter 3, God saved three of His followers from being burned in a fiery furnace by sending an angel to protect them from the flames. In chapter 6 of Daniel, God saved Daniel from being killed in the lions' den by sending an angel to shut the lions' mouths. In the New Testament book of Acts, chapter 12, an angel helped the apostle Peter who was in prison and facing a possible death sentence. He was being guarded by 16 solders and was made to sleep between two of them, bound with chains on his wrists. An angel woke up Peter in the middle of the night and removed his chains. The angel told Peter to get dressed and follow him out of the prison. After the angel helped him get safely away from the prison, the angel disappeared. God sent angels to protect His people.

A woman I go to church with shared a great example of protecting angels. She had been at a family wedding in a large town away from home. It was getting late, and she decided to drive back to the motel. At the parents' request, she took her grandchild along back to the motel with her. She stopped at a red traffic light, and when the light turned green, the car wouldn't move forward. She looked down to see that her foot was mysteriously pressing the brake pedal, not the gas pedal. Just then, a car went speeding through the intersection, through the red light. If she had pulled out when the light turned green, she would have been smashed by the speeding car that didn't stop for the red light. She was sure that an angel guided her foot to protect her and her grandchild. God sends His angels to do His work, and by doing so, He demonstrates His love for us!

The third angel task is giving encouragement and guidance to God's people. In Genesis 21, we learn about Hagar the servant woman, who had run away from her mistress. The angel of the Lord appeared to her and told her that she should return to her mistress and submit to her. He also told her that she would have a son and that her descendents would be too numerous to count. These statements gave Hagar guidance and encouragement. In Daniel chapter 10, an angel touched Daniel and gave him strength when he was weak. In First Kings chapter 19, God sent an angel to feed and encourage Elijah when he was hiding in the desert. In Matthew chapter 4, Jesus was in the desert for 40 days being tempted by the devil, and angels were sent to attend to Him. In Luke, an angel appeared to Jesus in the garden of Gethsemane to strengthen and encourage Him before He was arrested and eventually killed (see Luke 22:43).

Let me share with you a story that shows how God still uses angels to give guidance. Carol is a woman who has been an encouragement and a comfort to me since grade school. In 1970, she was living next door to a family that she had become very close too. At the time of this incident, she was nine months pregnant. Someone ran to her house one day and screamed that her neighbor's house was on fire. She ran outside to see smoke pouring out of the house. Carol knew that the 90-year-old grandmother was usually home during the day, so Carol pounded on the door, but there was no answer. She opened the door, and the combustion threw her backward to the ground.

The wife of the house was out canvassing the neighborhoods for the federal census, and Carol had no idea where she would be. Our town has nearly 20,000 residents and covers a large area. She prayed that God would guide her to wherever her friend was in the city. She drove directly to a side street where she had never been before and found the woman's car. She then asked God to show her which house the woman was in. The wife came out and they then drove back to the house. Thankfully, the grandmother was not in the house at the time of the fire, and Carol and her baby weren't hurt when she was knocked down. When the woman asked Carol how she knew where to find her, Carol told her that she prayed to God for guidance and drove directly to the spot. Carol said that her hands were on the steering wheel of the car but that she is sure an angel was really in control. God sends His angels to encourage and guide us today!

The fourth angel task is carrying out punishment. We have to remember that angels are very powerful and can kill a person quite easily if they are so instructed. Second Peter 2:11 tells us that angels are strong and powerful. In Second Samuel chapter 24, King David sinned, and God was angry with him because of his pride. As punishment for David's sin, God sent one angel who killed 70,000 people in three days with a plague. Our God is a loving God, but He is also a just God who promises consequences for sin, even if there is forgiveness. In Acts, chapter 12, God sent one of His angels to carry out a punishment. When King Herod was addressing the people, they yelled that he was a god and not a man. Because Herod didn't give praise to God, an angel of the Lord struck him down, and he was eaten by worms and died. There are many other instances in the Bible when God sent an angel to carry out His punishment.

The fifth angel task is patrolling or observing the earth for God. In Zechariah 1:7-17, we read that the prophet saw a man riding a horse and that there were other horses with him. The prophet questioned the angel who was with him about what this meant:

> I asked, "What are these, my lord?" The angel who was talking with me answered, "I will show you what they are." Then the man standing among the myrtle trees explained, "They are the ones the Lord has sent to go throughout the earth." And they reported to the angel of the Lord, who was standing among the myrtle trees, "We have gone throughout the earth and found the whole world at rest and in peace" (Zechariah 1:9-11).

In the book of Exodus, God sent an angel with the children of Israel to be on patrol with their army. The angel would move from one area to another as they needed him (see Exod. 14:19; 23:20,23; 32:34; 33:2). In Revelation, chapter 14, three angels were sent out to patrol the earth and to proclaim messages from God. In all of these examples, we find God sending out His angels to move about the earth, to observe it, and to patrol it.

The sixth angel task is fighting evil. Sometimes this is done to accomplish protection for God's people. Sometimes fighting evil is done to bring punishment. Sometimes it's for other purposes. God's angels also fight evil in response to our prayers. Daniel had been praying and fasting for three weeks when an angel appeared to him in a vision.

> *Then he continued, "Do not be afraid, Daniel. Since the first day that you set your mind to gain understanding and to humble yourself before God, your words were heard, and I have come in response to them. But the prince of the Persian kingdom resisted me twenty-one days. Then Michael, one of the chief princes, came to help me, because I was detained there with the king of Persia. Now I have come to explain to you what will happen to your people in the future, for the vision concerns a time yet to come"* (Daniel 10:12-14).

This passage shows us that sometimes, when we pray, we are causing a spiritual battle to take place out of our sight. This particular battle continued for 21 days before the angels defeated the demons and came to talk to Daniel. I think this explains one of the reasons why we don't always get immediate responses to our prayers. We also read a lot about angels fighting the forces of evil in the book of Revelation, "And I saw an angel coming down out of heaven, having the key to the Abyss and holding in his hand a great chain. He seized the dragon, that ancient serpent, who is the devil, or Satan, and bound him for a thousand years" (Rev. 20:1-2).

The seventh and final angel task is worshiping and praising God. As the psalmist wrote, "Praise Him, all His angels, praise Him, all His heavenly hosts" (Ps. 148:2). In Luke chapter 2, the angel told the shepherds about the birth of Jesus. When he finished telling them the good news, he was joined by a large number of other angels and they praised God together: "Suddenly a great company of the heavenly host appeared with the angel, praising God and saying, 'Glory to God in the highest, and on earth peace to men on whom His favor rests'" (Luke 2:13-14).

In the book of Revelation, God's angels continually praise and worship Jesus in Heaven:

> *Then I looked and heard the voice of many angels, numbering thousands upon thousands, and ten thousand times ten thousand. They encircled the throne and the living creatures and the elders. In a loud voice they sang: "Worthy is the Lamb, who was slain, to receive power and wealth and wisdom and strength and honor and glory and praise"* (Revelation 5:11-12).

> *All the angels were standing around the throne and around the elders and the four living creatures. They fell down on their faces before the throne and worshiped God, saying: "Amen! Praise and glory and wisdom and thanks and honor and power and strength be to our God for ever and ever. Amen"* (Revelation 7:11-12).

We are told in Revelation that, at the end of this world, God is going to banish the devil and all of his demons forever. At this time, the angels will no longer have to attend to God's people because we will live together with God in Heaven. According to Revelation chapter 7, it appears as though the angels will then have the pleasure of praising and worshiping God for eternity.

GOD, NOT ANGELS

God uses angels to talk to people in many different ways. When looking at the stories from the Bible, we find that often an angel encounter makes people afraid or fills them with awe. Their judgment occasionally becomes clouded, and they sometimes worship the angel instead of the One who sent the angel. During John's visions of the end-time, he bowed down to the angel who was showing him these things.

> *I, John, am the one who heard and saw these things. And when I had heard and seen them, I fell down to worship at the feet of the angel who had been showing them to me. But he said to me, "Do not do it! I am a fellow servant with you and with your brothers the prophets and of all those who keep the words of this book. Worship God"* (Revelation 22:8-9).

The apostle Paul also warned us not to worship angels (see Col. 2:18). We are also told in Exodus 20:3-4 that we should not bow down to anything in Heaven or on earth except God. We must remember that, although angels are powerful and have the ability to help us, they are only servants of God and can do only what He wants them to do. To worship them or pray to them would be taking the glory away from God.

GOD, NOT SATAN

Picture that old cartoon again. We just examined the role of the angel in white on the one shoulder. If we want to be realistic, now we have to talk about that little red guy on the other shoulder. A good place to start is Ephesians 6:10-12:

> *Finally, be strong in the Lord and in His mighty power. Put on the full armor of God so that you can take your*

stand against the devil's schemes. For our struggle is not against flesh and blood, but against the rulers, against the authorities, against the powers of this dark world and against the spiritual forces of evil in the heavenly realms.

We are reminded here that our true enemy is not evil people, but the evil forces around us, working in and through people who are disobedient to God. (Also see Ephesians 2:2.) This is hard to grasp because most people can't see the spirit world fighting against believers, just like we usually can't see angels fighting for us. That doesn't make any of these things less real than they are; they are just harder to discern or identify.

In his letter to the Ephesians, Paul warned them that the evil forces are arranged like an army. There is a definite chain of command, with the devil as the leader. We also read in Daniel, chapter 10, that certain demons are assigned to certain areas. It is wise to understand that the enemy that we are up against is not fighting in a haphazard way but is following a concise battle scheme! God's army of angels are also organized through a chain of command, with God as the leader. Only two good angels are named in the Bible—Michael and Gabriel. We are told in a few places that Michael is an archangel, or chief angel, and is in charge of other angels.

In Revelation chapter 12, we find that the devil, or satan, could very well have been an archangel at one time, because he was also in charge of other angels. We are told in Isaiah 14:4-15 and Ezekiel 28:11-19 (and in other places) that satan's downfall was pride. He wanted to be equal to or better than God. Because of this sin, God used Michael the archangel to throw the devil and his fallen angels (demons) out of Heaven (see Rev. 12:7-9). We also read in Jude 6 and Second Peter 2:4 that these angels will be punished in hell for eternity at the end of this world.

When satan was thrown out of Heaven for his sin, he took one-third of all the angels with him (see Rev. 12:4). These fallen angels joined him in his rebellion and are the demons that do his work. Revelation 12:9 tells us that satan and his demons try to lead the world astray. They want to prevent anyone from having a saving relationship with the Lord. If a person does have a relationship with God, the devil will try to destroy it. If the devil finds that he can't prevent or destroy our relationship with God, then he tries to distort and weaken it so that we are not as useful to God as we could be.

We can be encouraged to know that satan's demon army is not as strong as God's army of angels. "You, dear children, are from God and have overcome them, because the One who is in you is greater than the one who is in the world" (1 John 4:4). It's also nice to remember that God's angels outnumber satan's demons two to one. So not only is God much more powerful than the devil, but He also has him severely outnumbered! We also read in Romans chapter 8 that, in "all things," God works for the good of those who love Him. Later in the chapter, Paul wrote that neither angels nor demons can separate us from the love of God that is in Christ Jesus our Lord. Unfortunately, though, this doesn't mean that the devil and his cohorts won't stop trying. On the contrary, they will harass us even more when we believe in God and start yielding to Him and applying His rules to our lives. First Peter 5:8 says that we should be alert because the devil prowls the earth like a roaring lion, looking for someone to devour.

The devil tempts us when we are most vulnerable, just like a lion preys on the most vulnerable animal. When we are alone, or not in fellowship with other Christians, we are vulnerable. When we are at a physical high or low, we are vulnerable. When we are at a spiritual high or low, we are vulnerable. And when we are at an emotional high or low, we are vulnerable. The devil uses these times to tempt us in countless ways. He loves to manipulate us through our needs, desires, and emotions. He wants us to give up on God and God's way of doing things and to give in to him and choose the wrong way.

Satan has always wanted to be like God, and so we find in Second Corinthians 11:14 that he will "masquerade" as an angel of light and that his servants will do the same thing. We see this happen when any person or religion twists the meaning of Scripture or tries to appear religious while not accepting or believing who God really is and what He has done for us. When Jesus was being tempted by the devil in the desert, the devil quoted Scripture to try to get Him to sin. While the devil quoted the verses correctly, he twisted their true meaning. The devil and his demons know the Bible better than we do because they are powerful beings. Be assured, the devil continues to twist Scripture to implement his lies today.

One of the ways satan commonly twists the truth with believers is by giving the gospel first and then following it with the law, which is backwards of what God does. This is how it works. When a person is tempted to sin, the devil will tell them that it is OK-they can sin because God will forgive them (gospel). After they sin, he tells them they are worthless sinners who have broken the commandments (law), which then leaves them feeling guilty and hopeless. As we can see from the layout of our Bible, God gives us the Old Testament law first and then follows it with the good news of the New Testament gospel. When we are tempted to sin, the Holy Spirit tells us the law, that it is wrong to break God's commandments. If we do end up sinning, He gives us the gospel, that if we ask Him He will forgive us our sins and cleanse us from all unrighteousness, which leaves us with peace and hope. By simply changing the order of the law and the gospel, the devil is able to keep scores of people bound up in sin and feeling so guilty and hopeless they want to run from God. They are then not only kept from enjoying an intimate relationship with Him, they are kept from carrying out the work He has for them to do here on the earth.

OUR DECISION TO MAKE

Each of us must decide who God really is and what He means to us. We have important decisions to make. Unfortunately, many people don't realize that their decisions have eternal consequences. We will either be in Heaven or hell for eternity. The devil will try to deceive people about who God is right up until the time that they die or this world ends. If people think that they don't have to make a decision about who they believe God is, they have already made their decision. The Bible helps us make decisions and gives us the tools to discern the things we read or hear. John wrote about how we can be discerning:

> *Dear friends, do not believe every spirit, but test the spirits to see whether they are from God, because many false prophets have gone out into the world. This is how you can recognize the Spirit of God: Every spirit that acknowledges that Jesus Christ has come in the flesh is from God, but every spirit that does not acknowledge Jesus is not from God. This is the spirit of the antichrist, which you have heard is coming and even now is already in the world* (1 John 4:1-3).

We also find more guidance in First John 3:10, "This is how we know who the children of God are and who the children of the devil are: Anyone who does not do what is right is not a child of God; nor is anyone who does not love his brother." This second verse can't be taken out of context. It is not saying that if someone sins, they aren't or can't be a child of God. We know from other passages that we all have sinned. This is an area that the devil loves to use against us. The word *satan* means "accuser or slanderer."[1] He is very happy when he can tempt a Christian into sinning. Then he uses the sin to make the Christian feel guilty and to give non-Christians the opportunity to think that Christians are hypocritical. "...For the accuser of our brothers, who accuses them before our God day and night, has been hurled down" (Rev. 12:10).

The prophet Zechariah recorded the following vision:

> *Then he showed me Joshua the high priest standing before the angel of the Lord, and Satan standing at his right side to accuse him. The Lord said to Satan, "The Lord rebuke you, Satan! The Lord, who has chosen Jerusalem, rebuke you! Is not this man a burning stick snatched from the fire?" Now Joshua was dressed in filthy clothes as he stood before the angel. The angel said to those who were standing before him, "Take off his filthy clothes." Then he said to Joshua, "See, I have taken away your sin, and I will put rich garments on you"* (Zechariah 3:1-4).

Zechariah's vision should cause us much joy. We, like Joshua, stand before the Lord in our filthy garments, stained by sin, while being accused by the devil of our wrongdoing; yet the Lord offers us His cleansing forgiveness through His mercy and grace! Praise God for His undeserved love!

The next areas we will discuss about the devil and his demons are profound, yet they are rarely talked about. When we read the first few chapters of the book of Job, we learn some interesting things about the devil. He can't read our mind or truly tell the future, but he can sometimes guess what we are thinking and guess the outcome of a situation because he is very intelligent. In this book of the Old Testament, we find that he is accountable to God in all that he does and that he can't do just any old thing he wants to. Ephesians 1:20-23 explains how this also applies to the new covenant. It says that, once Jesus rose from the dead, all things were placed under His feet. This includes the devil and his demons, and it shows that they continue to be under the Lord's authority. Although the devil and his demons are under the authority of God (just like we are), we can't say that everything they do is in His perfect will, (in the same way that not everything we do is in God's perfect will). It is truly a mystery as to the seeming paradox of God honoring free will and yet at the same time being sovereign and completely in control, whether in the demonic realm or human realm for that matter.

In Luke 22:31 Jesus said, "Simon, Simon, Satan has asked to sift you as wheat." So the devil was asking God for permission to do something. In this case we see again that God was in a position to limit what the devil could do. There have been times when I have wondered, *If God is really a loving God, why did He allow this or that to happen?* Many people have wondered about this throughout the years. But God has eternity in mind in everything that goes on. He always desires the best for us in the long run, although our sin and the bad decisions we and others make at times interfere with the way His "perfect" plans are carried out.. Because we are trapped in our mortal bodies here on earth, and because we are not all-knowing like God, it is very difficult and sometimes impossible for us to see what God is able to accomplish despite the detours of heartache and tragedy in this life. When Jesus was crucified, His followers were mortified, even though He had told them what would happen. It wasn't until He had risen from the dead that they began to understand God's eternal plan.

The tragedies and difficulties that you and I deal with are no different than those of the disciples. We often have a hard time seeing the good that can come out of a tragic situation. This is when we have to have faith in God and His promises. We must believe that God has the ability to use all things for His eternal plan and His glory. Sometimes things that the devil and his demons do, are not only allowed by God—but are seemingly initiated by Him as a consequence for not submitting to Him and His rule. An example is in First Samuel 16:14-15, "Now the Spirit of the Lord had departed from Saul, and an evil spirit from the Lord tormented him. Saul's attendants said to him, 'See, an evil spirit from God is tormenting you.'" If we continue reading the book of Samuel, we find that God was not only punishing Saul, but also used this situation to get King Saul acquainted with the shepherd boy, David. David saw what it took to run a country, and he eventually became king.

Another example of God allowing an evil spirit to carry out judgement can be found in First Kings 22:19-23:

> *Micaiah continued, "Therefore hear the word of the Lord: I saw the Lord sitting on His throne with all the host of heaven standing around Him on His right and on His left. And the Lord said, 'Who will entice Ahab into attacking Ramoth Gilead and going to his death there?' One suggested this, and another that. Finally, a spirit came forward, stood before the Lord and said, 'I will entice him.' 'By what means?' the Lord asked. 'I will go out and be a lying spirit in the mouths of all his prophets,' he said. 'You will succeed in enticing him,' said the Lord. 'Go and do it.' So now the Lord has put a lying spirit in the mouths of all these prophets of yours. The Lord has decreed disaster for you."*

Again we see that God was able to use an evil spirit to accomplish something for Him. The Bible tells us that God created all angels. This would then include the devil and his group of fallen angels before they fell away. "See, it is I who created the blacksmith who fans the coals into flame and forges a weapon fit for its work. And it is I who have created the destroyer to work havoc" (Isa. 54:16). It is clear that the Lord is so completely sovereign that He is able to use even the bad things that the devil initiates and turn them around to accomplish His will in the end.

Let me give you a great example. I have spoken to numerous people in prison who have made this statement, "I found God only because I was put in jail. If I had never come here I would have never been forced to think about things like that." I fully believe it wasn't in God's "perfect" will for these people to be incarcerated, but because of the devil and the fallen nature it happened, and God ended up using the situation for their eternal good.

Only God knows what it will take to get a person or a nation to truly believe in and follow Him. Although not His perfect will, through the ages God has been able to use tragic situations to get people to seek Him because when everything is going well, we often think we don't need God. Many of us are so self-sufficient and self-reliant that it takes something completely out of our control to make us realize and acknowledge that we depend on God for everything, especially our very existence.

DECEIT

The devil lies to us. One of the main ways that he lies to us is by convincing us to seek out a source of power other than God. He tells us that, if we have a problem or a question, we can handle it ourselves; and if we can't, we can consult someone else—a worldly friend, our horoscope, a fortune-teller, medium, spiritist, anyone other than God. Because satan is powerful, he has the ability to perform amazing things through his followers, as seen in many false religions and in the occult. If someone does or says something miraculous, the power to do that feat came from either God or the devil.

But God makes it very clear in several places in the Bible that He is against anything involving the occult. "Do not turn to mediums or seek out spiritists, for you will be defiled by them. I am the Lord your God" (Lev. 19:31). God tells us the same thing again in Leviticus 20:6, "I will set My face against the person who turns to mediums and spiritists to prostitute himself by following them, and I will cut him off from his people." Further, Deuteronomy 18:10-12 says:

Let no one be found among you who sacrifices his son or daughter in the fire, who practices divination or sorcery, interprets omens, engages in witchcraft, or casts spells, or who is a medium or spiritist or who consults the dead. Anyone who does these things is detestable to the Lord, and because of these detestable practices the Lord your God will drive out those nations before you.

Dabbling in or using the occult is a very serious offense to God—He takes it as an open rebellion against Him. Satan is the source of power for these practices, so when we engage in them, we truly are teaming up with the devil, even if we don't realize it.

Another area in modern times that satan has gotten away with—for the most part undetected—is physical ailments and diseases. There are several instances in the New Testament when a demon or evil spirit was the cause of a physical problem such as being deaf, mute, blind, lame, or epileptic. While sometimes these ailments are caused by evil spirits, sometimes they're not. Jesus and His disciples saw a man who had been blind since birth. His disciples asked Jesus who had sinned, the man or his parents, that he had been born blind. Jesus told them that neither had sinned but the man was born blind so that the work of God could be displayed in his life. This blindness was not caused by an evil spirit but from some natural problem. Jesus healed the man and, therefore, displayed the love of God through the man's problem and eventual healing. (See John 9:1-5.)

In Mark 9:14-29, we read about an epileptic boy whom Jesus healed. Jesus said that a deaf and mute spirit was tormenting the boy. He cast the spirit out, and the boy returned to a normal state. In Luke chapter 13, we find a woman who had been crippled for 18 years. Jesus placed His hands on her and healed her. He told the people watching that satan had kept her crippled for all those years. This was another case of an evil spirit causing a physical problem, but God used the situation to reveal His love and glory. Mark 5:1-20 shows an example of how the devil uses his demons to cause mental problems. This still happens today. These problems can include many things like depression, insanity, anger, hate, rejection, jealousy, worry, confusion, split personalities, and even addictions, just to name a few.

Satan uses the same tactics and methods of operation now that he has been using ever since the Garden of Eden. First John 3:8 says that the devil has been sinning from the beginning of time and that Jesus came to destroy the devil's work. The devil used evil spirits to cause problems then and he does so now. But the good news is that God continues to perform miracles. I know people who have been healed from sickness, disease, and mental illness. Some problems were caused by evil spirits and some from natural causes. When a person has cancer, goes to the hospital, and is healed, we often say that it was a result of the miracle of modern medicine. Remember, God gave us "modern technology," and it is God who is in control of all things. These miracles still belong to God. When a person receives prayer from someone in a church service or elsewhere and is healed, it becomes very hard to give anyone but God the credit. God is in the miracle business, yesterday, today, and tomorrow!

The miracles that we see today are exactly what Jesus promised more than 2,000 years ago. In Mark chapter 16:15-18 Jesus said:

> *Go into all the world and preach the good news to all creation. Whoever believes and is baptized will be saved, but whoever does not believe will be condemned. And these signs will accompany those who believe: In My name they will drive out demons; they will speak in new tongues; they will pick up snakes with their hands; and when they drink deadly poison, it will not hurt them at all; they will place their hands on sick people, and they will get well.*

If we look at Jesus's words closely, we see that He claimed that His believers, or followers, will cast out demons and heal sick people, among other things. In Luke chapter 10, Jesus sent 72 messengers ahead of Him to every place that He was about to go. When the 72 returned, they told Jesus that even the demons submitted to them in His name. Jesus told them that He had given them the authority to trample on "snakes" and "scorpions" and to overcome all the power of the enemy. This power is available to us today!

EXPECT THE UNEXPECTED

One night, I attended a meeting at church where a woman told us about a mission project that she and her husband were involved with. After the meeting, I drove by the place where Lori and I had our van for sale. The Holy Spirit told me that we should give the van to the couple to help with the project. I immediately argued with the notion because we planned on using the money from the sale to go on vacation. When I got home, I told Lori about the mission project, and immediately Lori said we should give them the van to help fund the project. I began to cry because I realized that the Holy Spirit had told her the same thing that He had told me, but I had been too selfish to even mention it to her. We called the couple and explained our plan to them. They were very surprised, especially because just that day they had sold the husband's vehicle to purchase plane tickets for the mission trip. When they came to pick up the van, we had a chance to talk for a while and to get acquainted.

Before they left, they asked if we had any prayer requests that they could pray for us. I told them that I had been struggling with a drug addiction for nearly 20 years and would appreciate it if they kept me in their prayers. They looked at each other and then asked me a few questions. I told them that I often felt as if I had no choice and that I had to smoke pot to have any peace at all. What they said next surprised me. They said that it sounded like the demon of addiction had its grasp on me. I knew that I was addicted to drugs, but I didn't think I was controlled by a demon. They offered to pray for me. I told them that many people, including more than one pastor and priest, had prayed for me several times, but it had never seemed to help. They asked if anyone had ever tried to cast out an evil spirit or to release me from the grip of the demonic forces. I said no—and started to wonder just who these strangers were.

The four of us stood in a circle and held hands. The husband prayed first, and although my eyes were closed, I saw what looked like arms moving around my head. I thought the couple had let go of each other's hands and were moving their hands around my head for some reason. It began to distract me, and I started wishing that they would stop so that I could concentrate on the prayer. As the prayer continued, the arms moved more frantically, and I thought that my wife had joined in, but I refused to open my eyes. His wife started to pray, and the shadowy movements that I saw through my eyelids were moving so fast around my head that I couldn't separate them any more. She stopped praying to God, and then they commanded the evil spirits to leave in the name of Jesus Christ. Immediately, the shadowy movements were gone. They asked the Holy Spirit to come into me and my wife, and I could see that there was a bright light above us now. The couple stopped speaking, and I opened my eyes and looked up. I expected to see that the light fixture above had been turned on, but it wasn't— and everyone was still holding hands. They could tell that I was surprised and asked me what I was thinking. I told them about seeing the arms moving around my head. My wife said that she had seen the same thing but that she opened her eyes, and there was nothing there. I told them that I also saw a bright light after they demanded the evil spirits to leave and asked the Holy Spirit to come in.

I felt a great sense of peace that I couldn't explain, and so did my wife. When the couple left, Lori asked me if I felt the "electricity" coming through their hands like she did. I also had felt it and had noticed that Lori's hand had started to shake, which surprised me. Another thing that intrigued me was that, while the husband was praying, the wife had been very quietly speaking in tongues, and when the wife prayed, the husband also quietly spoke in tongues. It was only the second time in my life I had ever heard this before, and I was sure that my wife had never heard it. I asked Lori what she thought about the "speaking in tongues" stuff. She didn't know what I was talking about, so I showed her in the Bible what happened on the day of Pentecost. I explained that it was the strange language they were whispering as the other prayed. Again she said she hadn't heard anything odd. She said she heard the wife whispering but that the wife was saying "We love You, sweet Jesus," and "Come to us, Jesus," and things like that.

I could tell by the look in my wife's eyes that she was completely serious. I told her that I had heard the woman and man whispering but that it was in a language that I couldn't understand. I called the couple and asked the wife if they had been speaking in tongues when they were at our house. She said, "Of course." I asked her to talk to Lori. Lori had a puzzled look on her face after she hung up. I opened the Bible to First Corinthians chapter 12 and read to her the section about gifts of the Holy Spirit and that one of the gifts is interpretation of tongues. I explained to her that it was the only possible explanation for what she had heard compared to what I had heard.

The next day, we were attending a Bible study group, and we shared what had happened with the group. One of the members asked if I felt any different. I told her that I felt at peace and that I hadn't craved drugs at all that day. That night, when we went to bed, I had just turned off the light and started to pray when I heard the Holy Spirit speak very clearly to me. He asked me to recall a dream that I had had more than two years before. I had written the dream on my list, but I didn't need to look to remember the details. I began to shake violently as I recalled the dream (or what turned out to be a nighttime vision). I turned on the night light and tried to stand up, but I realized that my legs were shaking too hard. More than two years before it actually happened, God had given me a literal picture of the couple praying for me. It was so accurate that I saw the exact car they were driving. In my dream, they laid their hands on my head just as I had seen through my closed eyelids. For some reason, I didn't remember this vision until the Holy Spirit reminded me of it that next evening.

This one event has had a profound impact on my life. I am no longer addicted to drugs, I don't crave them, and I definitely don't feel like I can't survive without them. In addition, that day my wife and I both received a fresh in-filling, anointing, or baptism in the Holy Spirit (depending on the terminology you feel comfortable with). This has greatly enriched our marriage and lives. Almost immediately, God provided many opportunities for us to help others.

Casting out demons seemed strange to me at first, and if the same is true for you, I encourage you to please read the first four books of the New Testament and see how many times this issue is mentioned. If speaking in tongues is also strange to you, read First Corinthians and see what the Bible has to say to you. If you have any questions about the baptism or anointing of the Holy Spirit, read the book of Acts. These were all things that I had never been told about at church, but when I read the Bible, they are all in there.

SANCTIFICATION

Following my deliverance (the process of casting out demons), the Lord continued to teach me valuable lessons about sanctification. This is the on-going process of purging sin from a Christian's life.

In both Old Testament prophecy and New Testament fulfillment, we find that Jesus came to set the captive free. In John 8:1-11, Jesus rescued a woman from those who were about to stone her to death because she had been caught in the act of adultery. After saving her, the Lord told her, "Go now and leave your life of sin." Jesus set her free but admonished her to make better choices. If she decided to commit adultery again, she would be giving up her right to remain free or even to stay alive. The thought of a prisoner being released from jail and then returning by choice sounds ridiculous to us. But this is exactly what happens to many people.

I don't want to mislead anyone—my deliverance was nothing short of miraculous. The Lord completely removed from me the burning desire to do drugs. But I still had to contend with my sinful flesh, 20 years of habit, and a host of old friends who were still there to influence me. The Lord had not put up some force field around me that kept me separated from drugs; I had the free will to choose right or wrong. The Bible makes it clear that our struggle with sin is not a one-time decision, but an ongoing battle. First Thessalonians 4:1-3 says:

> *Finally, brothers, we instructed you how to live in order to please God, as in fact you are living. Now we ask you and urge you in the Lord Jesus to do this more and more. For you know what instructions we gave you by the authority of the Lord Jesus. It is God's will that you should be sanctified....*

But God is faithful, and as we seek to do what's right, we can rely on Him to help us through our day-to-day struggles. Philippians 1:6 tells us, "Being confident of this, that He who began a good work in you will carry it on to completion until the day of Christ Jesus."

FLEE TEMPTATION

The few times that I did smoke pot again after being prayed over became object lessons for me. The Lord used these times to teach me what would happen if I didn't avoid sin, sinful environments, and compromising situations. While I was in prayer after one of these episodes of defeat, the Lord gave me some insight into how to prevent this from happening again. He recounted to me the story of Daniel and the lions' den in Daniel 6. He showed me that every place where drugs are is a lions' den for me. He next told me that everyone has their own lions' den. Each of us has some area or areas where we are weak, and the devil is just waiting to pounce on us in those areas. Sometimes those areas are not even the real problem, but they are a symptom of some underlying problem that we need to acknowledge and fix with God's help.

The Holy Spirit showed me that God protected Daniel in the lions' den because Daniel was put there not by his own choice, but by the will of God. That was why, whenever I had to work in a place where people were doing drugs, God protected me and kept me strong just like He had protected Daniel. But when I chose to go into the lions' den on my own, like in a social setting, I was going in against God's will because God didn't want me there. He had already told me that more than once. It was at these times when God let the lions bite me because I was acting outside of His will. If we don't submit to God and His rule, we become vulnerable to evil and it's destructive effects on our life because we come out from underneath the umbrella of God's protection. To remain safe, we need to live within the boundaries placed in our lives by God.

I began to think about how this applied to people I know and their struggles. I have a friend who has a strong temptation to look at pornography. If he uses the computer when his wife is not home, he has a hard time not looking at pornographic sites. Cable television also can give him the opportunity to look at things that he shouldn't. For him, the lions' den is going on the computer or watching the television when he is alone. He knows what temptations are there and how hard it is to fight them. I have another friend who is dating a woman. He knows that God does not want them to have sex until they are married. But they love each other and they have already had sex, so it is a real struggle not to do so again. For him, the lions' den is staying at her house overnight or staying late enough that the kids have gone to bed.

If we are honest with ourselves, all of us can apply this truth to some area of our lives. We each battle with temptations of some sort, whether it be sex, sweets, or something else. Maybe we have friends with whom it is easy to gossip; maybe we are full of pride when it comes to talking about a certain aspect of our lives; or maybe we have a hard time not taking that second look at an attractive person of the opposite sex when we are notice them.. Your lions' den may not be as socially unacceptable as the next person's, or it may be worse. That doesn't matter because God tells us that all sin is wrong and separates us from Him. Of course, being tempted is not a sin. We have to give into our temptation before it becomes a sin.

But if we choose to put ourselves in a tempting situation, we shouldn't be surprised when we fail. It makes more sense to stay out of areas of temptation. There is no shame in running away. The apostle Paul mentored a young man named Timothy, and he told him (and us) more than once to "flee" from evil desires and temptations. In other words, run away from the lions and the lions' den whenever you can! The Lord showed me through a dream (and from experience) that, if we do find ourselves in the lions' den, we are to get as far away from the lions as we possibly can. Even if the lions' mouths are tied shut, it is still dangerous, and it would be unwise to be intrigued by the lions and to get too close to them. We don't want to instigate an attack—so we shouldn't pet the lions! But remember, if it is God's will for you to be in a certain area or place and you end up in the lions' den, you can be sure that He will offer you the protection that you need. He will either give you more strength or send His angels to close the mouths of the lions like He did for Daniel. You, like Daniel, have the choice to accept God's help or reject it.

In this chapter, we have looked at how God uses angels to carry out His will and to talk to us in our day-to-day lives. We have also discussed some of the different ways that God allows the devil and his demons to affect us here on earth. No matter what our circumstances, we can remember and believe what God tells us in Romans 8:28: "And we know that in *all* things God works for the good of those who love Him, who have been called according to His purpose."

YOUR TURN

Write about times in your life when you believe God has sent an angel to help or attend to you. It could have been in a physically or spiritually dangerous situation. You may have realized it was an angel at the time or you may not have realized it until later.

Write about times in your life when you saw or felt something that was so evil it had to be the work of the devil or one of his demons. We think of these things, not to dwell on them or glorify them, but to help us realize that there are truly evil forces in this world that we have to contend with.

STUDY QUESTIONS

1.   The Bible contains over three hundred references to angels, and it tells us that God made all of the angels (see Col. 1:16). What does the word *angel* mean? (See Daniel 4:13, and Psalm 103:20.)

2.   What is God's main purpose for sending angels? (See Hebrews 1:14; Psalm 34:7.) Compare the word *minister* as a noun and as a verb.

3.   What do you learn about angels from the old cartoon picture we keep mentioning, from my accident, and from Second Kings 6:14-18?

4. What do angels look like? (See Hebrews 13:2; and Isaiah. 6:1-2.)

5. Who is the angel of the Lord referred to in Genesis 22:15-18?

6. Do we have guardian angels? (See Matthew. 18:10.)

7. In what seven ways do angels accomplish God's will? (See the "Angel Encounters" section of this chapter.)

    a)

    b)

    c)

    d)

    e)

f)

g)

8. Why should we never worship angels? (See Revelation 22:8-9; Colossians. 2:18; and Hebrews 1.)

9. In the cartoon picture we keep mentioning, who is the little red guy on your shoulder? (See Ephesians 6:10-12; Daniel 10:12-14.)

10. Who is the devil, and who are his cohorts? (See Revelation 12:4,7-9.) What was his downfall? (See Matthew 4:1-11; Isaiah. 14:12-15; 2 Corinthians 11:14; and Ezekial 28:11-19.)

11. What does the word *satan* mean?

12. God gives us the law before the gospel. Why does the devil change this order and give us the gospel first and then end with the law? (See the "God not Satan" section of this chapter.)

13. What does it mean to us that satan is the father of lies? (See John 8:44 and the "Deceit" section of this chapter.)

14. When God created lucifer, He knew he would turn out evil in the end, but He still created him (see Ezek. 28:11-17). When He creates people He knows the ones who will not receive Him, but He still creates them. Does God value His decision to give us free will? Why?

15. Do we need to be scared? (See First John 4:4; Luke 10:19.)

16. Do we really trust the Lord? (See Romans 8:28.)

ENDNOTE

1. *Strong's NIV Exhaustive Concordance*, s.v. "satan."

JOURNAL

CONCLUSION

WHEN I STARTED WRITING THIS BOOK A FEW YEARS AGO, I thought that it was just going to be about the different ways God talks to people. What God has shown me during the writing process is that He had much more than that in mind for me to share. Here's a review of the eight chapters:

1. God talks to everyday people.

2. God talks through the process of prayer.

3. God talks through the Bible.

4. God talks through the spoken word.

5. God talks through the Holy Spirit.

6. God talks through design and circumstance.

7. God talks through dreams and visions.

8. God talks through angels.

When looked at as a whole, these eight truths are a complete picture of what a healthy relationship with God involves. He desires our relationship with Him to cover every area and aspect of our lives, including our waking and our sleeping. No wonder God uses the analogy of a husband and wife to describe our relationship with Him.

God is not a far-away deity in the sky. He is a real, living, active God. He is just as active today as He was when the Bible was written. He still talks to everyday people, and He wants to have a two-way relationship with us. He yearns for us to fall in love with Him like He has with us! To truly worship God is to have a close, intimate relationship with Him. To have that, we need to immerse ourselves in His presence and to spend time getting to know Him. This happens during prayer and praise; it happens when we read the Bible and study His Word; it also happens when we examine our lives and reflect on everything that He has done and is doing in our lives, because of the love He has for us. When we immerse ourselves in His presence, we will see so-called coincidences and fate for what they really are—God-controlled circumstances. We will realize that some dreams or visions that we have had were from God, to us and for us. We will also discern how we were, and are, protected by God during some physically or spiritually dangerous situations.

ONE-ON-ONE

As the Gospels prove, Jesus took the time to pray often. Ephesians 6:18 tells us to pray "on all occasions." First Thessalonians 5:17 tells us to "pray continually." When we start praying all the time, we will find that we aren't only asking God to grant our requests or to bless us. We end up just talking to Him and praising Him and thanking Him for being such a holy and awesome God. This leads us to start praying more often for His will to be done. Then when we do ask God for something within His will, and He grants it, then we will see it more clearly and appreciate it more dearly. This kind of constant, one-on-one time is more important to building our relationship with Him than reading any self-help book or listening to a sermon.

When you realize that the Maker of this universe really does love you and wants to have an intimate relationship with you, it is amazing! Your life will change, as will the way that you think about things and the way you live your life. A person who has this kind of close, healthy relationship with the Lord will find himself (or herself) wanting to go to church and do things to serve Him out of a spirit of praise and adoration. It will not be a duty or a chore, but a delight! Others will notice that there is something different about you—something desirable and appealing about you. When your old nature is put to death and you are submitting to your new nature, powered by the Holy Spirit, you become anointed to live the life that God desires for you.

If you desire to have a more intimate relationship with the living God, and you want to hear His voice, or hear it more clearly or more often, then you can follow the following ten biblical suggestions to help you on your journey. These are not ingredients to a magical formula; they are merely tools to help you consciously invite the Lord into every area of your life. Jeremiah 29:13 says, "You will seek Me and find Me when you seek Me with all your heart." Please remember that any steps that you take to get closer to the Lord should be done out of love and admiration for Him, not out of obligation, and definitely not out of a sense of justification. The Lord has shown me more than once that, when I do the right thing for the wrong reason, I am acting like the Pharisees of Jesus's day.

1. Humble Yourself Before God

This is critical if you want to have an intimate relationship with Him. Numbers chapter 12 tells us that the main reason that God spoke directly to Moses was because he was the most humble man alive. To truly humble yourself before God is to realize that no matter how "good" you are, it's not good enough to earn salvation or His love. These things are free gifts from His grace and mercy. Isaiah 64:6 says, "All of us have become like one who is unclean, and all our righteous acts are like filthy rags...." Romans 3:12 says much the same thing: "All have turned away, they have together become worthless; there is no one who does good, not even one." It is sad to say, but we still find today that many "church" people, among others, struggle with these facts just as they did in Jesus's time.

Proverbs 9:10 tells us, "The fear of the Lord is the beginning of wisdom, and knowledge of the Holy One is understanding." Psalm 128:1 states, "Blessed are all who fear the Lord, who walk in His ways." This kind of fear is a healthy fear, not a crippling fear. The Bible is describing a sense of reverence or awe for the Lord. It comes out of a humble attitude and from knowing that God is in control of everything and that we are accountable to Him for all that we do and say. He is Lord and Master of all, even if we don't know it or believe it.

2. Be Still Before the Lord

Psalm 46:10 says, "Be still, and know that I am God; I will be exalted among the nations, I will be exalted in the earth." In order to "be still" before God, we have to get rid of all other distractions. To help cultivate an intimate relationship with the Lord, we need to set aside some specific time each day when we can get rid of all the other background noises in our lives. These background noises may include television and radio, other people, the computer, the phone, and anything else that could distract you from hearing the Lord's gentle whisper. We read in the Bible that Jesus took time to be alone with God regularly; and if He had to, we certainly should as well.

3. Start Your Day With the Lord

God often speaks in Scripture about desiring our "first fruits." Getting into the habit of giving Him the first fruits of each day will help you dramatically in your journey toward hearing God speak to you. It sets the course for the rest of the day. Set up a steady routine that becomes a habit. I don't mean that you always say the exact same prayers and read the same verses every day but that you find a regular time and place to daily worship God and humbly await His voice. If you think that you don't have enough time to make this a daily habit, you need to understand its importance. We need to make time for God. God not only expects to come first in our lives, but He also deserves top billing. A relationship with Jesus Christ is the only thing that will fulfill our deepest longings here on earth, and it is the only thing that will get us into Heaven. What could be more important than that? This relationship makes the difference regarding where you will spend eternity. Submission to the Lord is a small price to pay considering that eternity lasts forever! "Teach us to number our days aright, that we may gain a heart of wisdom" (Ps. 90:12).

4. and 5. Thank and Praise Him Daily

Psalm 100:4 tells us to, "Enter His gates with thanksgiving and His courts with praise; give thanks to Him and praise His name." This tells us that we get through the "outer" gates by giving thanks. It tells us next that we get into His "inner" courts by praising Him. The second step (praise) is more personal than the first (thanksgiving), and it, therefore, moves us closer to God and connects us more intimately with Him, but both are important in a relationship with God.

6. Study the Scriptures

Reading the Bible during this personal time with God is critical. Through the Scriptures, you learn who He is and what He is all about. It is up to you how you choose to read the Bible—you can start at the beginning, the middle, or just open the Bible and begin where your eyes land. The method of choosing where is not as important as the act of actually doing it. You will be amazed at how often something you read in the morning will become relevant at some point during your day or in the very near future. God's Word is alive!

I have heard some people say that they don't know the Bible well enough to understand it, so they don't read it. This is like saying that a baby doesn't know how to walk so it shouldn't try. With the modern translations and study Bibles available today, most people can gain great understanding and work their way through the Bible with only a little effort. Of course, to maintain an honest perspective, we must understand that, as long as we are on this earth, we will never completely understand all of the mysteries of God. Because we are human, and He is God, we simply can't fully fathom how He thinks or acts.

> *For we know in part and we prophesy in part, but when perfection comes, the imperfect disappears. When I was a child, I talked like a child, I thought like a child, I reasoned like a child. When I became a man, I put childish ways behind me. Now we see but a poor reflection as in a mirror; then we shall see face to face. Now I know in part; then I shall know fully, even as I am fully known* (1 Corinthians 13:9-12).

7. *Daily Spend Time With God in Prayer*

An important aspect of our time with God is prayer, including prayers of thanksgiving and praise. After you have started in that fashion, you can move on to requests for others and also include prayers for your own concerns and for God's will to be done. When Jesus was asked how we should pray, He gave us one prayer that we can use as a pattern. It is a short prayer, but the individual petitions that make up the prayer can be used to guide us in all of our prayers. It is known as the Lord's Prayer:

> *Our Father which art in heaven, Hallowed be Thy name. Thy kingdom come, Thy will be done in earth, as it is*

in heaven. Give us this day our daily bread. And forgive us our debts, as we forgive our debtors. And lead us not into temptation, but deliver us from evil: For Thine is the kingdom, and the power, and the glory, for ever. Amen (Matthew 6:9-13 KJV).

8. Use a Daily Devotional

Although this is not talked about specifically in the Bible, many people find it helpful to use a printed devotional during their daily quiet time with God. Usually a devotional is a small booklet, divided into the days of the year, and each day contains some Scripture verses, a teaching or story and a prayer that relates to the Scripture. There are several daily devotionals available that cover an unlimited number of topics, styles, and even lengths. This is a matter of personal choice and is not mandatory to having a close relationship with God, although some people will find it helpful because it is structured and ties in certain Bible verses with a message.

Our Christian walk with God is a continual building up, or maturing, of our personal relationship with Him. We should not become stagnant in our union with the Lord; we should strive to progress. As Peter wrote, "But grow in the grace and knowledge of our Lord and Savior Jesus Christ" (2 Pet. 3:18). To be content with a mediocre relationship with God is to settle for something far less than what He offers us! We find in Ezekiel 37:1-14 a vision that the writer had about a valley full of dry bones. God showed Ezekiel that only He could bring the bones back to life. This analogy was initially about the children of Israel, but it also applies to us. If our relationship with the Lord can be compared to dry bones, we should not fear because the Lord can bring it back to life and make it better. We can ask God for this miracle, and He will answer our prayer as soon as we desire it and reach out to Him in faith.

Jesus said in Matthew 22:37-38 that the greatest commandment is to "Love the Lord your God with all your heart and with all your soul and with all your mind." He values our relationship with Him above all else! Jesus also said that, where our treasure is, there our heart will be also (see Matt. 6:21). He was talking about money at the time, but these words apply to other things as well, including our relationship with God. We each need to look at our own lives to see where our treasures are. Do we spend more time in a given week on our hobby, watching television, or performing some pleasurable activity than we do in cultivating our relationship with God? Where do we spend our money, and who gets paid first? These can be uncomfortable questions, but they also help identify our priorities— our "treasure."

A pastor once told me about a certain technique used for catching monkeys in Africa. A bucket is anchored to the ground, filled with raisins, and then covered with a lid that has a small hole cut in it. The monkey smells the raisins, comes down out of the tree, and then puts its hand into the bucket through the small hole. The monkey grabs a fist full of raisins, but with its fist closed, the monkey can't pull its hand back out of the small hole in the bucket lid and escape. The "monkey hunter" can then walk up and catch the monkey because it refuses to let go of the raisins. The monkey could remain free, but it chooses not to let go! How often are we like this monkey? The devil loves to trap us in much the same way, and therefore, we lose our freedom and miss out on the blessings that God has for us. It happens when we grab onto something in this world and refuse to let go, no matter what the cost; as Jesus says, it becomes our "treasure." Like the monkey, we often don't realize the danger of our actions!

Maybe it's something we do with our time that is valuable to us. At the end of the week, we may have spent more time watching television or doing a hobby than we have spent reading the Bible or praying. Maybe it's a sin that we have become comfortable with because we have justified it. We might say, "Everyone else is doing it, and besides, I don't see what is so wrong with it." Or we might say, "I deserve this." Or possibly we might say, "It's just the way that I am, I can't help it." Maybe it's our money that we can't let go of. We have worked hard for it, and it becomes very easy to claim it as our own, and therefore, we use it however we choose. We quickly forget that everything we have is on loan to us from God. For instance, name one possession that you can take with you when you die. The Lord says in Job 41:11, "Everything under heaven belongs to Me."

God tells us many times in the Bible that we will be rewarded when we "let go" of everything else and truly follow Him. Once our hands stop grabbing selfishly and we open them for Him, He can fill them with His blessings for us. "For the eyes of the Lord range throughout the earth to strengthen those whose hearts are fully committed to Him" (2 Chron. 16:9). So, each one of us has to ask ourselves, "Am I fully committed to the Lord?" Having a healthy relationship with the Lord doesn't happen by accident. It is intentional; we have to work at it and pursue it. We must make the choice to daily "die" to self and then "yield" to the Holy Spirit. This is what Galatians 2:20 means, "...I no longer live, but Christ lives in me...." When we start living for Christ, God will reward us with a friendship that is more exciting and fulfilling than most people ever imagine. It carries over into every area of our lives and changes us from the inside out. This kind of intimate union with God enables us to hear His voice often and gives us the ability to recognize or discern it.

If you were separated from a close friend while in a large crowd of people, would you recognize your friend's voice if he started calling out to you? Of course you would! Why? You know what his voice sounds like; you are familiar with it. Having a close relationship with God is like this. Life in general is like being in a crowded area. We have many distractions and things that are fighting for our attention. But when we have spent one-on-one time with God and know Him, we recognize His voice in the crowd, among the distractions of life. Jesus said it this way, "My sheep listen to My voice; I know them, and they follow Me" (John 10:27). It is comforting to know that, when we have this intimate relationship with God, not only do we know His voice, but He also knows us and our specific voices. Second Timothy 2:19 says, "Nevertheless, God's solid foundation stands firm, sealed with this inscription: 'The Lord knows those who are His,' and, 'Everyone who confesses the name of the Lord must turn away from wickedness.'" The second part of this verse brings us to our next step.

9. *Obedience to the Lord*

The Bible talks about obedience in many places. It is an essential aspect of our relationship with God. John wrote that it actually proves that we know Him, "We know that we have come to know Him if we obey His commands" (1 John 2:3). The more we truly get to know God and who He is, the easier it becomes to identify areas of inadequacy and sin in our lives. This is one reason why people refer to the process as maturing in the Christian faith. This is not to say that age alone promotes this; rather, time spent in earnest with God and our continued dedication to that relationship is the primary way to become mature in the Lord.

We know that the Bible says that we are all sinners. When we realize this important fact, we are on the right road to becoming humble, which leads to obedience. We will never be perfect while living on this earth, but that doesn't mean that we should not strive to follow God's will for our lives. The only way that we can do this is to daily crucify our old nature and to submit to our new nature. When we sin, we must ask God for forgiveness. Jesus died on the Cross to pay for our sin. He offers us forgiveness out of His love, His mercy, and His grace for us. After we have asked for and received His forgiveness, we need to make every effort to try to follow His will for our lives again. This is often a repeated cycle in the life of a

Christian; but as we mature, these cycles become less frequent. This is the sanctification process at work.

Our human nature and the devil tempt us to be disobedient. But faith in Jesus Christ as our personal Savior brings us salvation, and being actively obedient to Him proves that our faith is genuine. The Bible tells us that we can't earn our way to Heaven by following the rules but that our true faith in the Lord results in obedience and a changed life. We all have areas in our lives where we are tempted to sin. It is not easy to break an old habit or to change our way of life, but God gives us the strength to do just that. He offers help in various ways: through the indwelling power of the Holy Spirit, through the power of prayer, through Holy Communion, and through the fellowship of other believers. Regular church attendance can supply us with all of these things in one place at one time.

If you are dealing with a certain temptation, try to avoid any circumstance associated with it, if at all possible. Stay out of the lions' den if you don't want to be bitten! When we steer clear of tempting situations, it is easier not to fall into sin. Second Corinthians 10:5 says that another way to avoid sinning is to take every thought captive and make it obedient to Christ. This means that we try to stop a sinful thought pattern before it causes us to sin. For example, consciously not taking a second look at an attractive person of the opposite sex can prevent us from having a lustful thought, which could lead to a fantasy, which could lead to a sinful action. This takes empowerment from the Holy Spirit to work regularly and effectively in our lives.

It is possible that a prevailing sin that a person is dealing with may be there because a demon or evil spirit has its grasp on the person. God is able to free people from this power today, just like He did in the Bible. I have found that this situation is overemphasized in some circles and completely debunked in others. My belief is that we should take a biblically balanced approach to this subject. We need to be honest with each other and with ourselves. If something is simply a sinful work of the flesh, so be it; but if it is demonic in nature, we have to address that also. In either case, we are each responsible for our own sinful actions. I am delighted to tell you that, after my own "freeing" or "deliverance," I have had opportunities to watch other people set free from the bondage of evil forces. To see this happen with your own eyes is a kind of "spiritual reality check." To actually hear a demon speak from inside of someone is a sobering experience that can't be described with words.

Some people think that a Christian can't have a demon living inside of them. This train of thought says that demons can only affect Christians from the outside. I admit that I don't know everything, but I can tell you that I have personally heard demons speak from inside of people that I know are Christians. I have seen this and other physical manifestations of demons in Christians during the process of casting out the demons. I can't say that I fully understand how this works, but I believe it has to do with the fact that we are three-fold beings. First Thessalonians 5:23 tells us that we are made up of spirit, soul, and body. As Christians, we know that we are "possessed" or owned by God alone. Therefore the devil can not "possess" or own a Christian; but experience shows that a demon can inhabit our flesh, thoughts, and emotions once the door has been opened for them to come in.

I don't want to give him any more credit or attention than he deserves, but we need to remember that the devil and his demons are powerful and crafty. They are always trying to sway us off course so that we become lost or ineffective. As we talked about in the last chapter, the devil uses several tools to accomplish this. His strongest method of deceiving us also seems to be his favorite. It is when he uses a "truth" to implement his lie, therefore ending up with a "half-truth." Because there is an element of truth to his lie, it confuses us and makes his schemes and traps hard to identify.

If the devil can scare us or cause us to worry about a real situation or issue, he then plants a seed of doubt. Once we start doubting God or His mercy or His power, we are in big trouble! Sometimes the devil uses a passage of Scripture and then twists its true meaning or over-amplifies its importance relative to God's intended plan, he creates a false teaching. Many people with good intentions have been and are still being tricked by this deceptive tactic of the devil. Or, by getting us to focus on a real problem, tragedy, or difficulty, the devil leads us into depression and despair. Once we are weighed down with this load, we lose our hope and joy and become unable to help ourselves or anyone else. The devil will try to get some people to believe that they must rely on themselves for everything. When this self-sufficiency idea gets carried over into our spiritual lives, it leaves no room for the gifts of grace and mercy that are given to us through the death of Jesus on the Cross. It also negates an individual's empowerment, through the Holy Spirit, to live a sanctified life.

Truly, our real struggle is not against flesh and blood, but against the devil and all of his evil cohorts (see Eph. 6:10-18). Paul said in Ephesians 6 that we need to put on the full armor of God so that we can take our stand against the devil and his evil forces. The armor includes the belt of truth, the breastplate of righteousness, the gospel of peace, the shield of faith, the helmet of salvation, and the sword of the Spirit. We need to stay alert always and to pray in the Spirit on all occasions. When we put on the armor of God, we do not need to worry about the devil. The power of the Holy Spirit within us will enable us to overcome.

There are many things that the Holy Spirit can do for us, through us, and in us. Jesus told us that He would send the Holy Spirit to empower, guide, teach, and strengthen us. The Holy Spirit produces fruit in us, such as love, joy, peace, patience, kindness, goodness, faithfulness, gentleness, and self-control (see Gal. 5). The Holy Spirit also imparts gifts to us, including the gifts of teaching, prophesying, serving, encouraging, leading, healing, speaking in tongues, interpreting tongues, and distinguishing between spirits. While this is not an exhaustive list, it gives a good idea of how many different and varied gifts the Holy Spirit can give us. (See First Corinthians 12, Romans 12, and Ephesians 4 for the lists of spiritual gifts given in the Bible.)

All of these gifts and fruit are given to build up and mature the church. They prepare and empower us to be effective in our roles as members of the Body of Christ. Without an active empowerment of the Holy Spirit in our lives, we are ineffective, and our fleshly pursuits are futile. I encourage every believer in Christ to pray for a filling or anointing of the Holy Spirit. God loves to answer this prayer because it is in line with His will and glorifies Him. God can accomplish this filling several ways. The most important aspect is that we desire it. We can pray to be filled up, and after that, we can pray regularly to be "topped off." We can never have too much of the Holy Spirit! Ephesians 5:18 tells us to "be filled with the Holy Spirit." God talks to us most often through the Holy Spirit. Sometimes we quickly recognize that a certain thought came from Him while other times it can be harder to discern. The closer our relationship with Him is, the easier it will be for us to recognize Him when He speaks to us. Our Christian life evolves out of this relationship with God.

The apostle Paul, who wrote many of the books in the New Testament, compared the Christian life to running a race. In First Corinthians 9:24-27 and in First Timothy 4:7-10, Paul told us to go into strict training so that we might win the prize of eternal life. We do this when we cultivate our relationship with the Lord by spending time learning about Him, praying to Him, and praising Him. The writer of Hebrews (who many scholars believe to be Paul) told us to throw off everything that hinders us, and all of the sin that entangles us, so that we might finish the race as winners (see Heb. 12:1). We do this by taking our thoughts captive and by staying out of the lions' den. We also become winners by relying on His power to help us lead moral lives because we aren't able to be obedient on our own. In Philippians

3:13-14 and in Second Timothy 4:7-8, Paul demonstrated perseverance, writing about pressing on and straining toward the goal of finishing the race to win the prize of eternal life. This tells us that being a Christian won't always be easy. We will have to buckle down and fight the forces of evil with all of the tools and weapons that God gives us so we can live in victory. (I go into this subject in great depth in my book "A Miraculous Life".) Although this will sometimes be quite a struggle, the prize is worth the effort!

10. *Fix Your Eyes on Jesus*

Hebrews 12:2-3 says,

> *Let us fix our eyes on Jesus, the Author and Perfecter of our faith, who for the joy set before Him endured the cross, scorning its shame, and sat down at the right hand of the throne of God. Consider Him who endured such opposition from sinful men, so that you will not grow weary and lose heart.*

The admonition to fix our eyes on Jesus could very well be the most valuable piece of advice the Bible gives us. Our Lord and Savior is the only person that we can truly count on in this life. At some point, our health will fail us. Other people will let us down. Our circumstances will turn sour. We will find that we can't even count on ourselves sometimes. When these things inevitably happen, we can always turn our eyes toward Jesus. He is forever faithful and loving. Our survival as Christians depends on our knowledge of the value of this truth. We can't rely on emotions or feelings but only on the facts of who Jesus is and what He has done for us. "Who is it that overcomes the world? Only he who believes that Jesus is the Son of God" (1 John 5:5).

You probably know someone who doesn't believe that Jesus is the only way to eternal life in Heaven. Maybe you don't even believe it.

The Bible has this to say about the subject, "For the message of the cross is foolishness to those who are perishing, but to us who are being saved it is the power of God" (1 Cor. 1:18). Jesus told people that He was God. He said if they couldn't believe Him just because He said it, that they should believe Him because of the miracles that He did (see John 14:6-14). In Hebrews 2:3-4, we read that God the Father testifies to the message of salvation through Jesus by way of various signs, wonders, miracles, and gifts of the Holy Spirit.

This truth still applies to people today. Miracles are still being performed in the name of Jesus, and they remain proof that He is God. If you aren't sure, seek Him out and see for yourself! We can't demand that God perform a miracle for us as a sign, but we can pray for and expect an all-powerful God to do miracles that are of His will. God is not prejudiced. He offers His greatest miracle, the free gift of eternal life, to all who believe.

Jesus said, "People will come from east and west and north and south, and will take their places at the feast in the kingdom of God" (Luke 13:29). Focusing on Him could be visually represented by the Cross. The details of Luke 13:29 could be represented by a compass. If we superimpose these two images, we see that they blend perfectly together. (See the Sweet Bread Ministries' logo in the back of the book.) The Cross is our true compass and guide. Only when we align our lives with the Cross can we go in the right direction in life. When we are going in the right direction, we will have peace and joy that defy this world's reason and logic. When we are aligned with God's will for our lives, we are operating in spiritual balance because we are aligned with the pure truth of the Cross.

The north-south or vertical line represents our relationship with the Lord. When we are in line with Him and connected to Him, we can then have real and meaningful relationships with other people. The east-west or horizontal line represents these relationships with other people. If our alignment with God is off, we can see how it also affects our horizontal relationships. Anyone who has ever used a compass in the great outdoors can tell you that you have to look at it often to stay on track, because the terrain keeps changing. So it goes with daily life—our surroundings and circumstances keep changing, so it's easy to get off track or out of alignment with God and not even realize it! This is why it is imperative that we stay in close contact with the Lord. Our daily relationship with Him keeps us in alignment with His will for our lives.

If you ever try to use a compass inside a building or close to a large metal object, you will find that the compass needle goes awry. Pilots and other long distance travelers can tell you what a big difference only one or two degrees make when time and distance are involved. It could mean making a large detour or possibly not arriving at your destination at all. This is precisely what the devil and his companions are trying to do—they want to get us off center from God's will and to eventually take our eyes off Jesus. They know that even a slight deviation from the pure truth can have drastic effects over time. When satan is able to consistently manipulate us into making decisions and judgments based on "half truths," we encounter unnecessary difficulties and run the risk of becoming lost. There are religions and people worldwide who are using a compass that is not aligned with God's pure spiritual truth; these travelers will not arrive at the same destination as those who are focused on Jesus.

Maintaining alignment with God and His will is the only way to stay "spiritually balanced" in this life. It is a constant struggle and daily battle that we must consciously decide to fight. But when we have cultivated an intimate relationship with the Lord, we will be able to discern His voice through the several ways that He talks to us. By submitting to Him, we are then able to lead a truly balanced life and remain in His will for us.

PROCESSING WHAT YOU HAVE LEARNED

Throughout this book, I have tried to highlight the main ways and times that God has talked to me and to others that I know. I pray that everyone who reads this book comes to the realization that God is still talking to everyday people, every day. He might talk in different ways and at different times, but the fact remains that He is talking to us. Find out what that sounds like, what that entails. In John 8:47, Jesus told us, "He who belongs to God hears what God says." Pray for discernment so that you have your spiritual eyes and ears open at all times. Then you will be able to see the everyday events of your life for what they really are—spiritual battles between good and evil. That old cartoon that I keep referring to really is a picture of the spiritual reality around us. There are angels and demons much closer to us than many people might think.

I encourage you to periodically look at what you wrote at the end of each chapter. Add to the lists as you journey on your way to through this life. Use these lists to remind yourself that God is specifically talking to you and that He desires a close relationship with you because He loves you!. It will strengthen your faith dramatically when you believe and acknowledge this truth! "When they saw the courage of Peter and John and realized that they were unschooled, ordinary men, they were astonished and they took note that these men had been with Jesus" (Acts 4:13). My prayer for all of the everyday, ordinary people who read this book is that, after you cultivate your own intimate relationship with Jesus, your life will be changed so dramatically that all who know you will be astonished and take note of your relationship with Jesus.

God talks to everyday people! Are you listening?

STUDY QUESTIONS

1. God talks to us through the process of prayer, the Bible, the spoken word, the Holy Spirit, design and circumstances, dreams and visions, and angels. When seen as a whole, these truths are a complete picture of what a healthy relationship with God involves. Why do you think He talks to us in so many different ways? (See John 3:16; 6:45.)

2. How many of these ways can you relate to currently? (See John 8:47; 10:27.) Are there some ways in which you don't currently hear God that you would like to? (See Acts 2:17-18; Luke 11:13.)

3. When asked what the greatest commandment was, what was Jesus reply? (See Matthew 22:34-40; and Deuteronomy 6:5-9.) Why is this so important? (See Jeremiah 29:12-14 and Second Chronicles 16:9.)

4. What does this greatest command take? (See Second Chronicles 7:14-15.)

■ a.

■ b.

■ c.

■ d.

5. Do you truly desire to hear the voice of the Lord in your life more often or more clearly? If so, in what ways is it going to cost you? (see Matthew 13:44-46; 16:24-27; Luke 9:23; also see the the interpretation of the foundation dream in the "Changed Lives" section of the "Dreams and Visions" chapter.

6. And what are the benefits? (See Matthew 11:28-30; Jeremiah 29:11; and Revelation 21:3-8.)

7. What happens to those who don't want Jesus to be their Lord and Savior? (See Revelation 20:15–21:8.)

8. What are the consequences of trying to live with one foot in the world and one foot in the Church? (See Hebrews 10:19-31.)

9. What is God's purpose behind all of this? (See John 3:16 and First Timothy 2:3-4.)

JOURNAL

_____

_____

_____

_____

_____

_____

_____

_____

_____

_____

_____

_____

_____

_____

_____

_____

_____

_____

_____

_____

_____

_____

_____

Conclusion

EPILOGUE

As the Lord talks to us, it is our job to listen. Understand that, if we choose to tune Him out, He will continue to reach out to us, but eventually we will have to deal with the consequences of disobedience. My accident, which I share in the beginning of the book, was such a consequence.

In the spring of 2006, roughly eight months before my accident, I was working at a job site and felt prompted to call a close friend of mine, Ryan Clark. He used to be one of the pastors at my church, but he had moved to a different state and is now the senior pastor at a church there. We were talking for a while when he interrupted the conversation and said that the Lord had just spoken to Him.

I asked, "Well what did He say?"

Ryan replied, "He said you're to be an evangelist."

I got off the phone and went behind the garage that I was working at and laid down prostrate before the Lord. I began to pray and told the Lord that, if He wanted me to be an evangelist, He was going to have to tell me, not Ryan. The Lord instantly replied, "Quit praying and stand up, RIGHT NOW. Go back in that garage and write down all the times I have already told you, but you have refused to listen!"

I went back in the garage and came up with almost two notebook pages worth of times and ways that the Lord had tried to lead me into full-time ministry. I was very close to being done with this book at that point, and I concluded that when the book was in the book stores, if it started selling well then I would go into ministry full time. I reasoned that because I was very active in church already, that was good enough for now. After all, I was the director of evangelism, a council member, and a Bible study leader. This was my selfish logic, but it was not obedience.

A few months later, we went on vacation to visit Ryan and his family in New York for the first time. While we were there, I attended a mixed-denomination pastors' meeting that they hold weekly at his church. One of the pastors who attends this group, Ralph Diaz, is known for having a strong prophetic gifting. During the meeting, he had some words from the Lord for me. He said that this book would become popular and that it would be a springboard for a powerful ministry that the Lord was raising up. He went on to say that I would be seeing angels in the near future and that, while I was there on vacation, I would meet someone who was anointed by the Lord and that they would be important in my future.

PROPHECY FULFILLED

Much of what he said has already come true. As you know, I did get to see those angels (although it wasn't quite in the way I imagined). The ministry has also officially started and is taking root around the world. While on that vacation, I did meet someone that has played a major role in my life.

Before we left for vacation, I had a dream from the Lord about a man, and in this dream, he and I were eating some sweet bread together. When I prayed for the interpretation of the dream, all I was given was that it somehow involved Pastor Ryan. I called him the morning that I had the dream and explained it to him. Like me, he didn't know what it was about.

When we arrived in New York, Ryan introduced me to several people. One of the people he introduced me to was the same man that I had seen in my sweet bread dream! It was Bruce Carlson, the man who, months later, would fly to Wisconsin and pray for my intestine to grow in length. When I met him, I had no way of knowing that the Lord was going to use him to heal me after a bad accident, but I did know that the Lord had shown him to me in that dream for some significant reason. This also fulfilled another part of the prophetic word that Ralph Diaz had spoken, the part about me meeting an anointed person that would be important in my future.

That summer, I began to have so many dreams that I filled up a whole notebook documenting them. Many dreams were about a future ministry, what it would look like, what it would accomplish, and the idea that it would come only after great struggles. My lack of obedience and my refusal to listen to what the Lord said in this area also surfaced in a lot of these dreams. Some dreams that I had were about my old lifestyle. I had been completely sober for some time, but I occasionally thought about how things used to be. The Lord explained that He wanted me to live a righteous life because of my love for Him, not just so that I could say I was following all the rules. When I felt like I was missing out on all the fun, I had completely lost sight of the purpose and reasons for my changed life. I also had several dreams about my business. The Lord showed me that it meant far too much to me and that it was the real reason I had refused to go into ministry. I got my self-worth and value from being good at my occupation, not from my relationship with the Lord. I highly valued being self-reliant and owning a successful business. Over and over, the Lord showed me through different dreams how it hurt Him that I was choosing something else over Him.

THE BIG QUESTION

Toward the end of that summer, something very strange began to happen. Various times, while praying or reading the Bible, I clearly heard the Holy Spirit ask me if I would die for the advancement of the Lord's Kingdom. It was such a pointed question, and so shocking to me, that I refused to reply. After some time I called Pastor Ryan and told him about what I had been hearing. He was surprised to find that I had refused to answer. Approximately a month after telling him about this, I was praying while taking a shower, and it happened again. This time the Holy Spirit told me that I had been given enough time to think about it and that I now had to answer the question. Before answering, I asked a question of my own. "Lord, how could my death ever be used to advance your Kingdom?" I received no reply. I got down on my hands and knees in the shower and began to sob. I thought about many things, and I finally answered. I told the Lord that I would die for the advancement of His Kingdom.

But I had one request; I asked that He would send Lori and the kids another husband and father that would love them even more than I did. The Lord instantly responded, "I will," and I knew that it was a done deal. I continued to cry as I thought about someone else's clothes in my closet, another man raising my children and enjoying my wife's company. I wanted some answers, and I asked the Lord again how my death could help advance His Kingdom. Now that I had answered Him, He answered my question. He replied that my death would help get the message of this book out. I thought of different scenarios, but I could not come up with anything that made any sense as to how this could be possible. Pastor Ryan was the only person that I told about what happened that day in the shower. I asked him to comfort my family with the Lord's promise to me, if and when anything happened.

Two nights before my accident, I came home after a long day of work, and the kids were already in bed. That day, I had taken apart the truck that ended up falling on me and then did another small job somewhere else. I was tired and hungry by the time I got home, and I was glad to see that Lori had made up a plate of supper for me. As I sat at the table eating my food in silence, Lori began to talk to me. What she said completely took me by surprise. She told me that I needed to end our business and quit working as a mechanic immediately. I asked her who was going to pay our monthly bills if I quit working. She told me that I was a hypocrite for not trusting God after all the times that she had heard me tell other people to trust Him. She went on to say that I was being disobedient to the Lord for not going into ministry and that I knew it.

I became angry and told her to just let me eat my supper in peace. Instead of stopping, she became more emphatic and continued to try to convince me to quit. I told her that it was easy for her to say these things because she wasn't the one who had to support our family. She pointed out that God would take care of us if we were obedient. I slammed my fist on the table and told her I didn't want to hear another word. She stood up and then asked me three times, "What's it going to take for you to be obedient?"

ANSWERS

Two days later, I found out what it was going to take for me to comply. The truck fell on me and changed my life in countless ways. I believe that the accident happened because my continued disobedience in this area had made me vulnerable to an attack from the devil. The question for me has been did God allow it to happen because He was honoring my free will or was it consequences for my willful disobedience. To me, it doesn't matter because I know the Bible says that the Lord is in control of all things. (See Ephesians 1:11;20-23 and Colossians 1:15-20; 2:9.) A few of the people that I have shared this whole story with have told me that they don't believe God would ever use physical means to discipline people. But, beside the several examples in the Old Testament, I can think of some New Testament stories that prove otherwise. In Acts 5, Ananias and Sapphira died because they tried to lie to God. In Acts 12 King Herod was struck down by an angel of the Lord and died as a punishment. In First Corinthians 11, some of the believers in the church at Corinth become weak or sick or even died as punishment for taking the Lord's supper in an unworthy manner. Likewise, Hebrews 12:5-6 (KJ/NKJ version) tells us that the Lord disciplines His sons in the following order, first chastening or simple instruction, then rebuking or verbally reproving, and finally scourging, which is physical discipline. This shows an ascending order with the last resort being physical. Just like any good and loving parent it appears that the Lord wants us to listen to simple instruction or even a loving rebuke so that no further discipline is needed. The most convincing proof for physical consequences from sin as a last resort might come from Revelation 2:20-23 where Jesus Himself says that He is going to cast a false prophetess onto a bed of suffering (NIV version) or onto a sickbed (NKJ version) because she refused to repent after He had given her time..

Please don't try to apply this to every tragedy in life. That would not be fair or accurate. Our heartaches, problems, and troubles are not always a punishment for our actions, but sometimes they are a consequence of our sin. If you lead a homosexual lifestyle and get AIDS, your disease is a consequence for your actions. If you do something illegal and are put in prison, it is also a consequence. We could think of several examples that would apply, as well as many that wouldn't. Above all, we need to remember that the Lord loves us even more than we love ourselves. If He does do something to discipline us, Hebrews chapter 12 tells us that He does it out of love and for our own good. We must remember also that the Lord is more concerned about our eternal destination than our earthly contentment. Verse 11 explains the reason for His discipline: "It produces a harvest of righteousness and peace for those who have been trained by it." Just like children with their parents, we have a choice as to how we respond to the Lord's discipline. We can think that we don't deserve it, we can be angry and resentful toward God, or we can accept it for what it is and allow it to help us.

Five or six months after my accident, the Lord explained some things about my experience to me. One day, while I was praying, the Holy Spirit reminded me of the day in the shower when I had told the Lord that I would die for the advancement of His Kingdom. God informed me that He had answered my request for a man that would love my wife and children more than I did. I was confused and told God that I didn't understand since I was still around. He then told me that I was the man. I now loved and appreciated my wife and kids more than I ever had before. It's true; since my accident, my priorities have completely changed, and I do value my family more.

The Lord went on to say that I had been misrepresenting Him when it came to the accident story and why it happened. I had already told several people that the Lord had asked me if I would die for the advancement of the Kingdom and that when I said yes, this accident happened soon afterward where I "died" until He sent His angels to save me. God explained to me that I had completely misunderstood the question. He said that when He kept asking me if I would die for the advancement of the Kingdom, He was not talking about a one-time physical death at all, instead He was asking me to die to self everyday. He was calling me to full-time ministry and in order to do it I needed to die to my own plans, agendas, and ideas, but I had continually refused to. The Lord also reminded me that He had sent my wife 2 days before the accident to try and change my mind, but again I had refused to. It was not God's perfect will for my accident to happen, but because He is such an amazing God He is able to make good come from bad, and because of all the miracles that happened surrounding my accident, millions of people have gotten to hear how real He is and how much He loves us, even when we are not doing what we are supposed to.

TRUSTING GOD

You read earlier in this book about several of the prayers that the Lord has answered in my life. Although I am alive, I have to tell you that there have been some prayers since my accident that the Lord has not answered at all yet or that He has not answered in the way that I wished. More than once, I have been in so much pain that I have found myself calling out to the Lord asking Him to take it away. On several occasions, He has told me to call other people to pray for me. The first few times that this happened, I have to admit that I became angry with God because of that answer. I couldn't understand why a "middle man" had to get involved before He would answer my prayer. The very first time it happened, I refused to comply and just kept praying by myself for a long time. The pain finally became unbearable, and I called out to God, "Why aren't you helping me?" He replied, "I told you what to do!" When I finally broke down and gave in, I had Lori call some people and ask them to pray for my immediate need.

The results were always the same. I would have relief within a very short period of time. This cycle repeated itself, and each time it did, I actually felt farther from God. It hurt my feelings that He was refusing to answer "my" prayers. When I finally quit pouting and asked God what was going on, He explained that this process had a few purposes. One purpose was to help me begin to understand the power of other people's prayers in my life. This process also benefitted the people that we asked to pray for me because they were able to see God answer their prayers. Time and time again, people have told us that it really built up their faith when they prayed for me and God answered so quickly. They also felt encouraged and useful when we gave them the opportunity to do their part in the body of believers. It has, in turn, helped Lori and me to become less independent and more connected to our fellow Christians. Although these instances of needing prayer for great pain ended after the first year of recovery, we have used this lesson to help us greatly with other needs in our ministry.

Another important lesson that God has taught us through this ordeal is the simple nugget of truth found in Philippians 4:4: "Rejoice in the Lord always. I will say it again: Rejoice!" It doesn't say rejoice when things are going well and your needs are fully met. Keep in mind that Paul wrote these words from prison. He says "rejoice in the Lord always." This meant, for us, that we had to rejoice in the Lord after I got hurt, when I was in the hospital, and when I was at home in great pain. This isn't something that we can do on our own, in the flesh. This happens only when we have submitted our lives to the Lord completely and are living a life guided and empowered by the Holy Spirit. Rejoicing through painful circumstances is something that goes against human logic and worldly thinking.

Romans 12:12 tells us, "Be joyful in hope, patient in affliction, faithful in prayer." There is a distinction between joy and happiness. Happiness depends on our circumstances, unlike joy which runs much deeper. Joy is the confident assurance of God's work in our lives, the knowledge that He is there for us no matter what happens. Happiness leaves us as soon as we encounter the unavoidable bad times in our lives; but joy has the ability to keep us content in Christ, regardless of our circumstances.

The Apostle Paul learned the secret of staying content, no matter what was going on in his life. This contentment was rooted in the foundation of his relationship with our Lord, Jesus Christ. Paul wrote, in Philippians 4:12-13, "I know what it is to be in need, and I know what it is to have plenty. I have learned the secret of being content in any and every situation, whether well fed or hungry, whether living in plenty or in want. I can do everything through Him who gives me strength." Experiencing this kind of joy and contentment in Christ doesn't happen overnight. It takes time to develop and nurture that kind of relationship with our Lord. After we do, however, these traits are imparted to us by the Holy Spirit living inside of us. As we grow and mature in the Lord, God guides and controls our lives more and more. We will increasingly live out the admonition, "Trust in the Lord with all your heart and lean not on your own understanding" (Prov. 3:5).

For the first few years after the accident, life as we knew it was only a memory. I was not physically able to do much of anything and I dealt with quite a bit of pain. But God has been faithful and I can say that at this point I have been not only healed but restored in nearly every way, physically and otherwise!

We had no disability insurance at the time of the accident and the bills began to pile up as I wasn't able to work for a few years. That being said, I must tell you that the Lord provided for and blessed our family through our church, friends, family, and community so much that we were completely taken care of during our time of greatest need. The amount of love that God has shown us through other people since my accident is completely overwhelming! Though it has been a hard road, my family and I can attest to the truth of the promises given in the Bible. The Lord is faithful, and He can be trusted! He really does love us more than we can ever imagine. Paul's statements about God-given joy and contentment in the midst of troubles are as true today as they were when he first wrote them. I encourage you to taste and see that the Lord is good! I pray the words of Romans 15:13 will ring true in your life: "May the God of hope fill you with all joy and peace as you trust in Him, so that you may overflow with hope by the power of the Holy Spirit."

TASTE AND SEE THAT THE LORD IS GOOD

THE SEVEN WAYS GOD SPEAKS TO US AND THE TESTIMONIES IN this book prove that Christians today can still have relationship, or covenant, with the living God found in the Bible.

The best part about entering into this relationship is not the benefits we have on this earth, although they are great. The best part is the assurance that, at the point of death, when we pass from this life into the next, we will spend eternity with the God who loves us more than we can imagine.

In order for that to happen, we need to know some things. First, we are all sinners, and sin cannot enter Heaven. Even if we are "good" people, it is not enough (see Rom. 3:20-23; 6:23). The good news is that Jesus died on the cross to pay the price for humanity's sins because of God's love for us (see John 3:16; Rom. 3:24-25).

The second part almost sounds too good to be true, but it is. Romans 10:9 tells us, "That if you confess with your mouth, 'Jesus is Lord,' and believe in your heart that God raised Him from the dead, you will be saved." If you have never asked Jesus to forgive your sins and come into your heart, and you are willing to make Him the Lord of your life, then just say these words from a sincere heart right now:

> *Dear Jesus, I know I am a sinner. I have sinned against You and other people, and I am sorry for my sins and repent of them. I ask for and receive Your forgiveness today. Jesus, I invite You to be the Lord and Savior of my life, and I believe in my heart You died for the penalty of my sin on the cross and after three days were raised from the dead and are now seated in Heaven. Lord, I ask You to send Your Holy Spirit to fill me to overflowing even now and to melt me, mold me, and shape me into the person You want me to be. In Jesus's name I pray. Amen.*

If you just prayed that pray and meant it, it is settled. You are now a child of God and are in covenant with Him. This is the absolute most important decision you will ever make, and whether you felt anything or not, you are now "reborn," as Jesus said in John 3.

This is just the start of a new and exciting life. To help you along that journey, here is a list of things you should do as soon as possible:

1. Find a church that teaches the Word of God and get involved.

2. Fellowship with mature believers who can help you to grow in your newfound faith.

3. Get water baptized and tell others what you have done.

4. Start reading the Bible daily and praying to God as you would talk to your best friend, knowing that He loves you.

5. Make the daily choice to live for God and honor Him through your obedience to Him and love for others.

Congratulations on your decision! You have experienced the greatest miracle possible and can now expect to have daily relationship with the One True Living God!

SWEET BREAD MINISTRIES IS A NON-DENOMINATIONAL MINISTRY dedicated to bringing people of all backgrounds into a closer, more intimate relationship with the Lord and the abundant life He offers us. We strive to do this through biblical preaching, teaching, prayer, and healing as well as orphanage support and free book ministry to jails and the poor. We are available to speak at your church, school, local correctional facility, or special event worldwide. We also offer one- and two-day seminars as well as prayer and revival services. Please contact us if you desire to see people get saved, healed, set free, and delivered by the power and love of Jesus.

SWEET BREAD MINISTRIES

230 State Highway 66

Rudolph, WI 54475

Phone: 715-213-6116

Website: sweetbreadministries.com

Email: questions@sweetbreadministries.com

In the right hands, This Book will Change Lives!

Most of the people who need this message will not be looking for this book. To change their lives, you need to put a copy of this book in their hands.

> *But others (seeds) fell into good ground, and brought forth fruit, some a hundred-fold, some sixty-fold, some thirty-fold* (Matthew 13:8).

Our ministry is constantly seeking methods to find the good ground, the people who need this anointed message to change their lives. Will you help us reach these people?

> *Remember this—a farmer who plants only a few seeds will get a small crop. But the one who plants generously will get a generous crop* (2 Corinthians 9:6).

EXTEND THIS MINISTRY BY SOWING
3 BOOKS, 5 BOOKS, 10 BOOKS, **OR MORE TODAY,**
AND BECOME A LIFE CHANGER!

Thank you,

Don Nori Sr., Founder
Destiny Image
Since 1982

DESTINY IMAGE PUBLISHERS, INC.

"Promoting Inspired Lives."

VISIT OUR NEW SITE HOME AT
WWW.DESTINYIMAGE.COM

FREE SUBSCRIPTION TO DI NEWSLETTER

Receive free unpublished articles by top DI authors, exclusive discounts, and free downloads from our best and newest books.

Visit www.destinyimage.com to subscribe.

Write to: Destiny Image
             P.O. Box 310
             Shippensburg, PA 17257-0310

Call: 1-800-722-6774

Email: orders@destinyimage.com

For a complete list of our titles or to place an order
online, visit www.destinyimage.com.

FIND US ON FACEBOOK OR FOLLOW US ON TWITTER.

www.facebook.com/destinyimage   facebook
www.twitter.com/destinyimage   twitter